T0132489

CREOLES OF SIERRA LEONE
PROVERBS ◆ PARABLES ◆ WISE SAYINGS

'Dèm Salone Créole Pipul Dèm Parεbul'

WITH LITERAL
ENGLISH TRANSLATION AND INTERPRETATION

EYAMIDÉ ELLA LEWIS-COKER

authorHOUSE®

AuthorHouse™
1663 Liberty Drive
Bloomington, IN 47403
www.authorhouse.com
Phone: 1 (800) 839-8640

Published by AuthorHouse 08/06/2018

ISBN: 978-1-5462-5273-3 (sc)
ISBN: 978-1-5462-5272-6 (e)

Library of Congress Control Number: 2018908681

Print information available on the last page.

Any people depicted in stock imagery provided by Getty Images are models, and such images are being used for illustrative purposes only.
Certain stock imagery © Getty Images.

This book is printed on acid-free paper.

CONTENTS

PARABLES ARE THE DAUGHTERS OF DAILY EXPERIENCE
'DƐM CREOLE GYAL PIKIN DƐM WE ƆNDASTAN PARƐBUL ƐN UZ DƐM ƐVRIDE FƆ MEK DƐM LAIF BETƐ'

INTRODUCTION

'Dèm Salone Créole Pipul Dèm Parɛbul'

CREOLES OF SIERRA LEONE
PROVERBS ♦ PARABLES ♦ WISE SAYINGS

Proverbs, parables and wise sayings are meaningful short sayings or vehicles through which morals are transmitted to adults, youth and children. They are daily life experiences that the Africans utilized to understand their past and present lives.

These means of expressions are genuinely significant to the African culture as they transmit wisdom, truth, morals and lessons which convey traditional views passed down from generation to generation.

Africans and mostly older Africans communicate to adults, youth and children by means of proverbs, parables and wise sayings; transmitting messages, imparting warnings, solving problems, influencing behaviors, helping to avoid unwanted outcomes and shaping or molding, especially the children as they journey through life.

Proverbs, parables and wise sayings are the instinctive or spontaneous methods of learning anywhere and anytime through conversations in an African community. As the conversations lag, they are revived by these short sayings. These modes keep the African children active and interested in the world around them, as well as their own development.

These short sayings, in simple terms are the daughters of daily life experiences. They are not explained after they've been expressed; instead adults, youth and children used them to improve their communication and listening skills, develop creative imaginative and thinking skills, understand the meaning of life and be familiar with the element of each proverb that was transmitted.

Proverbs, parables and wise sayings are the oral literature of the Creoles of Sierra Leone. Each proverb is understood when expressed in ordinary conversation.

The role and importance of proverbs, parables and wise sayings in each ethnic group of Sierra Leone conversations, provide a colorful and poetic picture of the African culture and its characteristics.

There are times when proverbs, parables and wise sayings are used to give warnings to husbands on how to live and rule their household.

In many ways proverbs, parables and wise sayings are used daily in modes that one cannot always express in normal conversations and sometimes when normal words, phrases or sentences cannot be expressed in ways you would like someone to understand them. In these cases you would use proverbs, parables and wise sayings.

Indeed, proverbs, parables and wise sayings in the Creole culture are used as guiding lights or stepping stones to the next generation. They come in handy during conversations and help family unite in their times of need.

In a point of fact, without the use of the ancestral proverbs, parables and wise sayings; the Creole culture would have lost much of its customs, morals, traditions and values.

'Dèm Salone Créole Pipul Dèm Parɛbul'

CREOLE PROVERBS ◆ PARABLES ◆ WISE SAYINGS

ABILITY, CAPABILITY, GIFT, OR TALENT

Parable or Saying: *Gɔd nɔ go gi yu lod wɛ yu nɔ go ɛbul fɔ tot.*

Translation: *God won't give you more than you can bear.*

Interpretation: God only gives you what you can handle. God is faithful; he will not let you be tempted beyond what you will endure.

ACCEPT THE FACT OR ACKNOWLEDGE THE FACT

Parable or Saying: *Wɛtin briz dòn blɔ, ĩ dòn blɔ.*

Translation: *Blown in the wind.*

Interpretation: Disappeared, gone forever or there is nothing you can do to solve the problem.

Parable or Saying: *Wɛ farinya ná basin fɔdɔm ná sansan, wɛtin yu go du?*

Translation: *It's no use crying over spilled/split farina.*

Interpretation: Do not worry about things that had happened. Let go!

Parable or Saying:	*Wɛ milk dòn trowɛ ná grɔn, wɛtin yu go du?*
Translation:	*It is no use crying over spilled/spilt milk. Crying will not retrieve the milk.*
Interpretation:	Don't express regret for something that had happened and cannot be remedied. Crying will not improve the situation. Give it up!

ACHIEVEMENT, ACCOMPLISHMENT, TRIUMPH OR SUCCESS

Parable or Saying:	*Kil babu sho mɔŋki.*
Translation:	*Slay a baboon and exhibit a monkey.*
Interpretation:	Someone who publicly parades his/her possessions or accomplishments.

ACTION, ACTIVITY, MANNER OR PERFORMANCE

Parable or Saying: **Kaw ol sotɛ, ĩ liba nɔ ol.**

Translation: *No matter how old the cow is, his/her liver is still functioning.*

Interpretation: A person should not underestimate the value of an elderly.

Parable or Saying: **Lɛ yu akshɔn tɔk pas yu vɔis.**

Translation: *Actions speak louder than voice.*

Interpretation: What you do is more important than what you say.

Parable or Saying: **Dèn sɛ wok ɛn gɛt kɔpɔ, yu sɛ lan buk.**

Translation: *Work and receive your pay check, stop bragging about your education.*

Interpretation: Knowledge is not the main thing, but deeds.

Parable or Saying: *Aw yu mɛk yu bed, ná so yu go lidɔm pan am.*

Translation: *As you make your bed, so must you lie on it.*

Interpretation: You are responsible for the consequences of your own actions.

Parable or Saying: *Akshɔn spik lauda dan wɔd.*

Translation: *Action speaks louder than words.*

Interpretation: Your intentions can be judged better by what you do rather than your statements.

Parable or Saying: *Yu an tu shɔt fɔ bɔks wit Gɔd.*

Translation: *Your hands are too short to box with God.*

Interpretation: You are too small to fully grasp God's greatness and don't argue with God because HE is your creator.

Parable or Saying: *Wɛtin yu so, ná im yu go rip.*

Translation: *Whatever you sow, you shall reap.*

Interpretation: You are responsible for the consequences of your own actions and the choices you have made.

Parable or Saying: *Assis go flai bak pan di pɔsin fes wɛ trowɛ di assis.*

Translation: *Ashes always fly-back on the face of the person who throws the ashes.*

Interpretation: Whatever you have done (good or bad), will have an effect on you. What goes around, comes around!

Parable or Saying: *Wɛ yu trowɛ assis, ĩ go fɔdòm bak ná yu fes.*

Translation: *When you throw ashes, ashes will fly-back on your face.*

Interpretation: You will always reap what you sow.

Parable or Saying: *Yu tek rop drɔ bush, naw bush dòn kam ná toŋ!*

Translation: *You took a rope to pull down trees in the forest, the forest is now in town.*

Interpretation: You have created the problem; to get rid of the problem is not easy. In some situations, the problem will bite you!

Parable or Saying: *Gro usai dèn plant yu.*

Translation: *Grow where you've been established.*

Interpretation: Do the best that you can, with what you can, while you can. Success is inevitable.

Parable or Saying: *Wɛ yu du gud, yu go gɛt di pɛ.*

Translation: *If you do something good to someone, sooner or later you will be rewarded either directly or indirectly.*

Interpretation: As we work to create light for others, we naturally light our own way. Those who persevere in doing good receive eternal life.

Parable or Saying: *Wɛ yu tif, yu go gɛt di pɛ.*

Translation: *Stealing has serious consequences.*

Interpretation: It is forbidden to steal, there are consequences for stealing.

Parable or Saying: *Wɛ yu bad, ná bad fɔ tek pul bad.*

Translation: *Do evil that evil may come.*

Interpretation: Repay evil with evil.

Parable or Saying:	*Gɔt kaka waŋ rɔl dòŋ il, ĩ de wet fɔ udat go push am.*
Translation:	*Goat excrete is anticipating to roll down a hill but waits for someone to shove it down the hill.*
Interpretation:	An impending event triggered off by an unintentional action.

Parable or Saying:	*Jɔj mi fɔ wɛtin á de du.*
Translation:	*Judge me by my actions or deeds.*
Interpretation:	You must judge a man by the work of his hands.

Parable or Saying:	*Yu si tide, yu nɔ si tumara.*
Translation:	*What you plant today, you will harvest tomorrow.*
Interpretation:	The best preparation for tomorrow is doing your best today.

Parable or Saying:	*Yu de si tide, bɔt wɛ tumara?*
Translation:	*What you plant now, you will harvest later.*
Interpretation:	The best preparation for good work tomorrow is to do good work today.

Parable or Saying:	*Wɛ yu pit ná grɔn, yu nɔ go lik am bak.*
Translation:	*If you salivate on the ground, you will not salvage it.*
Interpretation:	The words which proceed out of the mouth of a person come from the heart; and these defile a person. Be careful of what you say to others.

Parable or Saying:	*Udat lib bai di sɔd go dai bai di sɔd.*
Translation:	*If you live by the sword, you will die by the sword.*
Interpretation:	If you use violence against other people, you can expect to have violence used against you.

Parable or Saying: *Wɛ yu klem ɔp tik, yu gɛt fɔ kam dɔŋ di sem tik.*

Translation: *When you climb up a tree, you must descend from the same tree.*

Interpretation: If you get yourself in, you must be able to get yourself out.

Parable or Saying: *Wɛ yu dig grev fɔ yu ɛnimi, sɔntɛm de ná yusɛf yu de dig di grev fɔ.*

Translation: *If you dig a grave for your enemy, you better dig two.*

Interpretation: Expect that whatever evil you plan for someone is likely to happen to you.

Parable or Saying: *Á de kil tu bɔd wit wan ston.*

Translation: *Kill two birds with one stone.*

Interpretation: With just a single action, you manage to do two things at the same time.

Parable or Saying: *Kɔt yu kot akɔdin tu yu klos.*

Translation: *Cut your coat according to your cloth.*

Interpretation: Match your actions to your resources, and do not try to live beyond your means.

Parable or Saying: *Kɔt yu kot akɔdin tu yu shep.*

Translation: *Cut your coat according to your shape.*

Interpretation: Coordinate your acts to your assets, and do not try to live beyond your reserves.

Parable or Saying: *Les tɔk mɔ akshɔn.*

Translation: *Less talk more action.*

Interpretation: Action speaks louder than words.

Parable or Saying: *ɛvri dɔg gɛt in de.*

Translation: *Every dog has his day.*

Interpretation: Whatever goes around comes right back, so your actions are very valuable. Be careful of what you say or do because sometimes it comes right back at you.

Parable or Saying: *Bɔd waŋ flai yu go shek di tik.*

Translation: *A bird is anticipating to fly away then someone accidentally shakes the tree.*

Interpretation: An impending event triggered off by an unintentional action.

Parable or Saying: *Wɛ yu nɔ wok, yu nɔ go yit.*

Translation: *If you are unwilling to work, you will not eat.*

Interpretation: Someone who refuses to strive hard will not achieve his/her life goals.

Parable or Saying: *Tɔk nɔ go ful yu baskit ná fam, yu gɛt fɔ wok.*

Translation: *Talking will not fill your basket in the farm, you have to work to harvest the farm.*

Interpretation: Strive hard to accomplish your goals.

Parable or Saying: *ɛvride nɔto Sɔnde.*

Translation: *Everyday is not Sunday.*

Interpretation: You cannot rest everyday, sometimes you have to work.

Parable or Saying:	*Jɔj man ɔ uman bai di wok wɛ ĩ de du.*
Translation:	*You must judge someone by the work of his or her hands.*
Interpretation:	**Judge someone by his or her accomplishments.**

ADAPT, ADJUST, ALTER, MODIFY OR CHANGE

Parable or Saying: *Kɔmiɛl nɔ gɛt bɔks, bɔt ĩ de chenj ĩ klos.*

Translation: *The chameleon has no suitcase or portmanteau but he/she switches outfits.*

Interpretation: Someone who alters his/her behavior to suit the situation.

ADVANTAGE OR TO PROFIT SELFISHLY

Parable or Saying: *Wɛ yu briŋ sɔmbɔdi ná yu pala, ĩ go waŋ fɔ tek yu bedrum.*

Translation: *Invite a self-seeking person in your living room, he/she will try to occupy your bedroom.*

Interpretation: Just remove one space between the words "Someone" and "who"

Parable or Saying:	*Wε yu gi sɔmbɔdi lilibit, ĩ go waŋ fɔ tek ɔl.*
Translation:	*You give someone an inch, he will take a mile.*
Interpretation:	Someone who is achieving a selfish goal by exploiting a kind-hearted person.

Parable or Saying:	*Dèn de tek yu yon fat fɔ frai yu.*
Translation:	*They are taking your own grease to fry you.*
Interpretation:	One who habitually takes advantage of others kindness.

Parable or Saying:	*Ná rɔtin bɔdi blant Jizɔs.*
Translation:	*It is the rotten corpse that belongs to Jesus.*
Interpretation:	A person who depends on the charity of others for food, shelter, etc.

Parable or Saying:	*Wε yu lidɔm ná grɔn, sɔmbɔdi go waka pantap yu.*
Translation:	*If you lie on the floor someone will walk over you.*
Interpretation:	A person who allows someone to abuse, exploit, manipulate, misuse, impose or take advantage upon.

ADVICE, COUNSEL OR GUIDANCE

Parable or Saying:	*Pikin wε sabi was in an go yit wit dèm alagba dèm.*
Translation:	*If a child knows how to wash his/her hands, the child could eat with kings.*
Interpretation:	A young person who is disciplined and well-mannered will participate with elders.

Parable or Saying:	*Á tɔk tu yu, yu nɔ yɛri; ná di wud dat. Lonta!*
Translation:	*I had a long discussion with you, but you did not listen. Nothing further.*
Interpretation:	You do not take my advice; I have nothing further to say.

AFRAID, FRIGHTENED OR SCARED

Parable or Saying:	*Ĩ de fred lɛk pus.*
Translation:	*He is scared like a cat.*
Interpretation:	Someone frightened by almost everything.

Parable or Saying:	*Á nɔ gɛt lɔŋ tit fɔ saund 'S'.*
Translation:	*I do not have an extra-long tooth in my mouth to pronounce the letter 'S'.*
Interpretation:	Someone who is scared and always try to avoid an unwanted situation.

AGREE, BE TOGETHER, CONCUR
OR SEE EYE TO EYE

Parable or Saying:	*Wɛ yu fɔdɔm fɔ mi, á go fɔdɔm fɔ yu.*
Translation:	*If you assist me, I will assist you.*
Interpretation:	If you help me, I will help you or if you do me a favor, I will return the favor.

Parable or Saying:	*Wɛ yu krach mi bak á go krach yu bak.*
Translation:	*If you scratch my back, I will scratch yours.*
Interpretation:	If you do something for me that I cannot do for myself, I will do something for you that you cannot do for yourself.

Parable or Saying:	*Ná in finga de go insai mi nos.*
Translation:	*His/her finger is just right for my nose.*
Interpretation:	When two people agree on something or view something the same way.

Parable or Saying:	*Tu ed bɛtɛ pas wan.*
Translation:	*Two heads are better than one.*
Interpretation:	If two people work together or solve a problem together, the result will be better than having one person to solve a problem.

Parable or Saying:	*Ná tu an yu de tek fɔ kach lɔs.*
Translation:	*It takes two fingers to remove lice from a person's head.*
Interpretation:	Two people may be able to solve a problem than one person.

AGGRESSIVE, ASSERTIVE OR RUDE

Parable or Saying:	*Ĩ pit kɔla ná im mɔt wɛ ĩ bɔn.*
Translation:	*She spat chewed kola nut in the child's mouth when the child was born.*
Interpretation:	She uses forceful methods to succeed or to do something and she is ready and willing to argue or fight. She has a sharp tongue!

Parable or Saying:	*Ná im gbakanda!*
Translation:	*Someone who is aggressive.*
Interpretation:	Someone who is likely to attack or confront anyone.

Parable or Saying:	*Ná in tɔŋ shap!*
Translation:	*He/she has a sharp tongue.*
Interpretation:	Someone who says words that are unkind or harsh. A sharp tongue is like a sharp knife. It can slice the best in one's relationship.

Parable or Saying:	*Ná ayɛn yu de tek fɔ shap anɔda ayɛn.*
Translation:	*It's an iron that is used to sharp another iron.*
Interpretation:	A person sharpens the character of his/her friend.

Parable or Saying:	*Ná ayɛn yu de tek kɔt anɔda ayɛn.*
Translation:	*Iron cuts iron.*
Interpretation:	Refers to two people equally matched in intelligence, aggressiveness or cunning.

ALIKE, SAME OR SIMILAR

Parable or Saying:	*Mɔŋki tɔk, Mɔŋki yɛri.*
Translation:	*Monkey speaks; monkey understands.*
Interpretation:	People who think alike understand themselves.

Parable or Saying:	*Ná papa mɔŋki go mared mama mɔŋki.*
Translation:	*It is Master Old-Man Monkey who marries Misses Old-Woman Monkey.*
Interpretation:	People who do similar things in life and tend to share the same interests.

Parable or Saying:	*Di ren wɛ bit sugaken sotɛ ĩ swit, ná di sem ren bit bita lif sotɛ ĩ bita.*
Translation:	*The rain that beats sugar cane until it is sweet is the same rain that beats bitter-leaf until it is bitter.*
Interpretation:	Do not rejoice over someone's misfortune, because the same everyday problem that a person is facing today could happen to you tomorrow.

Parable or Saying:	*Da ship wɛ briŋ baibul, ná di sem ship briŋ rɔm.*
Translation:	*The ship that brought Bible was the same ship that brought rum, whisky, liquor or alcohol.*
Interpretation:	A good person who is betrayed and easily angered would be the revengeful type. The same person who is good can be evil.

Parable or Saying:	*Wɛ yu ná drunko, drunko, yu go tink lɛkɛ drunko, drunko.*
Translation:	*He, who drinks alcohol, thinks like an alcoholic.*
Interpretation:	People with the same or some of the same characteristics.

Parable or Saying:	*Di apul nɔ fɔdɔm fawɛ ná di tik.*
Translation:	*The apple doesn't fall far from the tree.*
Interpretation:	A child who inherits his/her parents' traits (good or bad).

Parable or Saying:	*Di apul nɔ fɔdɔm fawɛ ná di tik.*
Translation:	*The apple doesn't fall far from the tree.*
Interpretation:	Like father like son.

Parable or Saying:	*Di apul nɔ fɔdɔm fawɛ ná di tik.*
Translation:	*The apple doesn't fall far from the tree.*
Interpretation:	Like mother like daughter.

Parable or Saying:	**Bɔd wɛ gɛt di sem fɛda, gɛda togɛda.**
Translation:	*Birds of the same feather flock together.*
Interpretation:	People who are a lot alike tend to gather together and become friends.

AMBITION, ASPIRATION, DESIRE, DREAM OR GOAL

Parable or Saying:	*Magomago.*
Translation:	*A person with too much ambition will not sleep in peace.*
Interpretation:	Excess ambition that involved anger and jealousy is dangerous.

Parable or Saying:	*Yu nɔto lesman bikɔs yu trai ɛn fel.*
Translation:	*To try and fail is not laziness.*
Interpretation:	You've tried your best and failed but at least you've achieved something.

Parable or Saying:	*Wɛ yu ep yusɛf, Gɔd go ep yu.*
Translation:	*God helps those who help themselves.*
Interpretation:	*If you want to succeed, you must make the effort.*

Parable or Saying: *Wɛ yu waŋ fɔ klem lɛda, bigin ná di bɔtɔm*

Translation: *When you want to climb a ladder, you must start at the bottom.*

Interpretation: To gain high status, you must start with a low position and slowly work upwards to be successful.

Parable or Saying: *ɔri, ɔri bɔs trɔsis.*

Translation: *You hurry until you ripped your pants.*

Interpretation: If something is done too quickly, it may be done carelessly and need to be redone.

Parable or Saying: *Wɛ yu lɛf fɔ drim ná im dat!*

Translation: *If you cease to dream, you will cease to live.*

Interpretation: Without dreams to dream, a person's life becomes meaningless.

Parable or Saying: *Wɛ yu waŋt yu eg fɔ ach, sidɔŋ ná di eg.*

Translation: *If you want your eggs to be hatched, you have to sit on the eggs.*

Interpretation: Protect your area until you are ready to emerge or become known.

Parable or Saying: *Wɛ yu wok, yu go gɛt wɛtin yu waŋt.*

Translation: *Strive hard to accomplish your dreams.*

Interpretation: It takes determination and hard work to accomplish your goals.

Parable or Saying: *Tek tɛm kil anch, yu go si in gɔt.*

Translation: *Take your time to exterminate an ant, you will see its intestines.*

Interpretation: Accomplishing one's ambition through diligence.

Parable or Saying:	*Wɛ yu waŋ go ɔp, no usai yu de go.*
Translation:	*People with goals succeed because they know where they are going.*
Interpretation:	The journey to success starts with knowing the end-goal. All you need is a plan, a road map and the courage to press on to your destination.

ARGUE, DISPUTE OR QUARREL

Parable or Saying:	*Wan an banguls nɔ de shek.*
Translation:	*A single bracelet does not shake.*
Interpretation:	It takes two to argue or quarrel.

ARROGANT, BIGHEADED, CONCEITED, CONDESCENDING OR PROUD

Parable or Saying:	*Dèn sɛ wok, yu sɛ yu go Grama skul.*
Translation:	*Strive very hard to accomplish your dreams instead of bragging about your education.*
Interpretation:	Common sense is better than formal education or learning.

Parable or Saying:	*Buk lanin nɔto kɔmɔn sɛns.*
Translation:	*Education does not result in common sense.*
Interpretation:	It is not because someone is educated he/she has common sense.

ASSISTANCE, AID, BENEFIT, COMFORT, HELP, RELIEF OR SUPPORT

Parable or Saying:	*Wε yu nɔ kɔl sɔmbɔdi fɔ opin yu dɔmɔt, udat go opin am?*
Translation:	*If you fail to call someone to open your door, who will open your door?*
Interpretation:	The only way to get help is to ask someone.

Parable or Saying:	*Wε yu nɔ kɔl fɔ sɔmbɔdi, udat go opin yu do?*
Translation:	*Unless you call out, who will open your door?*
Interpretation:	If you don't ask for assistance, you may never get one. People around you are there to help.

Parable or Saying:	*Lubi nɔto slev ná drɔsup, ná obligeshɔn ī de du.*
Translation:	*Rock potash when added in okra soup is owing it a favor to make it thick and slimy.*
Interpretation:	A helping hand cannot be expected to assume full responsibility.

Parable or Saying:	*Jakas bɔn im pikin fɔ lε ī blo.*
Translation:	*Jackass delivers her child so that she will rest.*
Interpretation:	To help someone in need or support someone.

ASSOCIATION OR CONNECTION

Parable or Saying:	*Bɔd dèm wε fiba de togεda.*
Translation:	*Birds of the same feather flock together.*
Interpretation:	People tend to associate with those of similar character, interests or opinions.

ATTACH, AFFIX, CLIPPED OR CONNECT

Parable or Saying: *Wɛ yu ná kɔp andul, yu gɛt fɔ tek tɛm.*

Translation: *If you are the cup handle, beware of the cup.*

Interpretation: Work with your spouse as a team and set your family values. Set your boundaries and limits with your in-laws. Be at your best behavior around your in-laws.

AVOID, EVADE OR REJECT

Parable or Saying: *If yu nɔ waŋ lɛ mɔŋki tel tɔch yu, nɔ go ná mɔŋki in dans.*

Translation: *If you do not want the monkey's tail to touch you, do not attend the monkey's dance.*

Interpretation: A person might avoid unwanted outcomes by not participating in an invent.

Parable or Saying: *Mi ná Jon bad ed, á nɔ de go jakato fam.*

Translation: *John who is always blame for something bad will not visit the garden eggs' farm because garden eggs are sometimes destroyed by frost in cold weather.*

Interpretation: A person who is always accuse of being responsible for something bad will avoid visiting a challenging area.

BAD, AWFUL, CORRUPT, EVIL, TERRIBLE OR WICKED

Parable or Saying: *Bad tik nɔ go bia gud frut.*
Translation: *A bad tree cannot bear good fruit.*
Interpretation: Parents with behavior problems do not raise good children.

Parable or Saying: *Ná bad wokman di tɔk bad bɔt in tul.*
Translation: *A bad workman always blames his tools.*
Interpretation: Blaming tools for bad workmanship is an excuse for lack of skills.

Parable or Saying: *Bad yai nɔ di si ɛnitin gud.*
Translation: *An evil eye sees no good.*
Interpretation: An evil eye is a look that is known to be able to cause injury or bad luck for the person at whom it is directed.

Parable or Saying: *Bad bush nɔ de fɔ trowɛ bad pikin.*
Translation: *There is no undesirable forest to cast a bad child.*
Interpretation: A child with bad behavior should not be disowned. Parents should try to shape a child's behavior.

Parable or Saying: *Fisha-man ɔ fisha-uman nɔ de sɛ in fish rɔtin.*
Translation: *A fishmonger will not say all his fish stink or rotten.*
Interpretation: A person will never talk badly about his/her behavior or character.

Parable or Saying:	*Wε yu lidɔm wit dɔg, yu go grap wit fli.*
Translation:	*If you lie down with dog, you will get up with fleas.*
Interpretation:	If you are around bad friends, you will be influenced by them and you will get into trouble.

Parable or Saying:	*Opin ɛnemi bɛtɛ pas bad frɛn.*
Translation:	*Open enemy is better than bad friend.*
Interpretation:	It's better to know who your real enemies are rather than trust someone who pretends to be a friend but is capable of stabbing you in the back.

BAD CHARACTER, CROOK, OUTLAW OR ROGUE

Parable or Saying:	*Yu kɔba smok sotε, ĩ go mɔs kɔmɔt.*
Translation:	*No matter how you try to cover up smoke, it will come out.*
Interpretation:	A person's bad character will be revealed at the appropriate time.

BAD SITUATION

Parable or Saying:	*Yu kɔmɔt ná frai pan, yu go ná faya.*
Translation:	*Jumping from the frying pan into the fire.*
Interpretation:	Escaping a bad situation to a worse situation.

Parable or Saying:	Kongosa kin prɛd kwik.
Translation:	*Bad news travels fast.*
Interpretation:	People are quicker to pass on bad news than good news.

Parable or Saying:	*ɛlifant ed nɔto pikin lod.*
Translation:	*The elephant's head is no load for a child.*
Interpretation:	When a situation is bad, any chance at relief is good.

BEAUTIFUL, ATTRACTIVE, FINE LOOKING, GOOD LOOKING OR GORGEOUS

Parable or Saying:	*Fayn ná fes nɔ to di tin, ná gud trik.*
Translation:	*Beauty is skin deep.*
Interpretation:	Looks are superficial, sometimes a beautiful person may have unpleasant characteristics.

Parable or Saying:	*Fayn ná fes nɔ to di tin, ná gud trik.*
Translation:	*Beauty is in eyes of the beholder.*
Interpretation:	Different people see beauty in different ways. What one person finds beautiful may not appeal to another person.

Parable or Saying:	*Nɔ to ɛvritin wɛ de shayn ná gol.*
Translation:	*All that glitters is not gold.*
Interpretation:	Things that appear on the surface to be of great value may be quite worthless.

Parable or Saying:	*Nɔ to ɔl fayn apul gud.*
Translation:	*Not all pretty apples are good.*
Interpretation:	Not everything that looks precious turns out to be good.

Parable or Saying: *Wɛ fayn uman fayn, ĩ fayn.*

Translation: *A pretty woman does not need to try to be pretty.*

Interpretation: *She is pretty; she has love, understands; she respects herself and others; everyone likes, loves and honors her; she is a goddess.*

Parable or Saying: *Fayn uman ná wahala.*

Translation: *He who marries a beauty, marries trouble.*

Interpretation: Everyone admires a beautiful woman without a good character.

Parable or Saying: Ná yu waŋ si sɛ di pɔsin fayn.

Translation: *Beauty is in the eye of the beholder.*

Interpretation: The perception of beauty is subjective, and not everybody finds the same people or things attractive.

BEHAVIOR, CONDUCT OR MANNERS

Parable or Saying: *Wɛtin pikin tɔk ná trit, Ĩ don yɛri de sem tin ná ose.*

Translation: What a child says, he has heard at home.

Interpretation: The way a child behaves in public largely reflects the kind of job his parents had done in bringing him/her up.

BELIEVE OR ACCEPT AS TRUE

Parable or Saying: *Wɛ á si, á go biliv.*

Translation: *Seeing is believing.*

Interpretation: I have to see it to believe it.

Parable or Saying: *If mi yes nɔ yɛri, mi at nɔ go pwɛl.*

Translation: *If I do not hear, it won't spoil my heart.*

Interpretation: If a person doesn't know about something, it won't hurt them.

Parable or Saying: *If tapoŋ tɛl yu sɛ kuta in bɛlɛ de at am, biliv am bikɔs ná dèn ɔl de ɔnda di wata.*

Translation: *If a tarpon tells you that a barracuda has an upset stomach believe because both of them live underneath the sea.*

Interpretation: If a person with experience explains a particular subject that you know nothing about and he/she has evidence to back it up, believe and trust that person.

BEST, FINEST, GREATEST OR TOP

Parable or Saying: *If yu sɛ ná trit yu go de klin, klin am gud.*

Translation: *If your job is to clean the streets, clean the streets perfectly.*

Interpretation: Do what you love to do and give it your best.

BLOOD, DESCENT, FAMILY, HERITAGE, ORIGIN

Parable or Saying: **Blɔd tik pas wata.**

Translation: *Blood is thicker than water.*

Interpretation: Relatives before friends.

Parable or Saying: **Kenkeni fambul blɔd bɛtɛ pas impɔrtant fren.**

Translation: *An ounce of blood is worth more than a pound of friendship.*

Interpretation: Take care of your relatives before friends.

Parable or Saying: **Blɔd tik pas wata, bɔt wata tes bɛtɛ.**

Translation: *Blood is thicker than water, but water taste better.*

Interpretation: Sometimes interacting with friends or strangers is less stressful than interacting with problematic or difficult relatives.

Parable or Saying: **Fambul ná lɛk tik, ĩ kin bɛn bɔt ĩ nɔ de brɔk.**

Translation: *Family tie is like a tree, it can bend but it cannot break.*

Interpretation: Family members are related for better or for worse.

Parable or Saying: **Nɔ was yu fambul dɔti linin ná trit.**

Translation: *Home affairs are not talked about on the public square.*

Interpretation: Family should remain confidential amongst family unless it is life threatening.

Parable or Saying:	*Wɛ brɔda dèm fɛt tɛ dèn kil dèmsɛf, ná trenja go gɛt di prɔpati wɛ dèm papa lɛf fɔ dèm.*
Translation:	*When brothers fight to death, a stranger will inherit their father's estate.*
Interpretation:	Brothers should solve their problems without violence, because a stranger will be the receipient of their inheritance from their father.

BRAG, BOAST OR SHOW OFF

Parable or Saying: ***If yu yams wayt, kɔba am.***

Translation: *If you have white yams, conceal or hide them.*

Interpretation: Do not impress others with your dressing, speaking style, walking style or intelligence. You do not know what the future holds.

Parable or Saying: ***Nɔ prez yusɛf.***

Translation: *Do not sing your own praises.*

Interpretation: Let someone else say good things about you but not from your own mouth.

Parable or Saying:	*Nɔ blɔ yu yon ɔn.*
Translation:	*Do not blow your own trumpet or horn.*
Interpretation:	Allow someone else to tell the world about your accomplishments.

Parable or Saying:	*Sol nɔ de prez insɛf ná sup.*
Translation:	*Do not boast.*
Interpretation:	Let someone announce to the world about something that you have achieved successfully.

Parable or Saying:	*Bos, bos nɔ gud bikɔs ná lilibit yu go ɛbul du.*
Translation:	*He who boasts a lot does little.*
Interpretation:	To talk, act or write about oneself or something related to oneself in a proud or self-admiring way.

Parable or Saying:	*Big mɔt!*
Translation:	*Big mouth or loud mouthed person.*
Interpretation:	You talk and brag too much; especially about things that should be secret.

Parable or Saying:	*Poman gɛt ɔg ed ĩ ɛng am ná fɛnch fɔ drai.*
Translation:	*He speaks of his accomplishments.*
Interpretation:	He brags to win the approval of others so that he will feel alright about himself.

Parable or Saying:	*Yu ná tɔk, tɔk! Yu ná awoko!*
Translation:	*You talk to much and never shut up!*
Interpretation:	Stop talking about what you want to do in life, you need to start to do it!

Parable or Saying: **Tɔk, tɔk bɔd nɔ de bil ose.**

Translation: *A chattering bird builds no nest.*

Interpretation: Stop talking about what you want to do in life. You need to start it! If you don't start, you will never have what you want.

Parable or Saying: **Layon wɛ de mek nɔis nɔ de kil natin.**

Translation: *An ounce of someone's family blood is worth more than a pound of friendship.*

Interpretation: You cannot gain anything by sitting around talking about it. You must get up and work for it.

Parable or Saying: **Pus wɛ de mek nɔis nɔ de kach arata.**

Translation: *A meowing cat catches no mice.*

Interpretation: You cannot achieve or gain anything by mere sitting around and just talking about it.

Parable or Saying: **Wɛtin yu de sɛ at fɔ du.**

Translation: *Words are easily said than being in charge.*

Interpretation: Something that a person says to some degree seems like a good idea but it is difficult to do.

Parable or Saying: **Nɔ tɔk di tɔk wɛ yu nɔ ɛbul fɔ wok di wok.**

Translation: *Don't talk the talk if you can't work the work.*

Interpretation: Don't boast of something if you are unwilling or unable to back it up by your actions.

Parable or Saying: **Awoko; tɔk, tɔk pɔsin.**

Translation: *Very talkative person without action.*

Interpretation: Those people who have a little knowledge usually talk the most and make the greatest fuss.

Parable or Saying:	***Dadi ɔ mami tɔk, tɔk.***
Translation:	*A talkative person without action who has little concept of when it would be appropriate to keep quiet.*
Interpretation:	**A person who only talks or perhaps talks big and don't do anything.**

Parable or Saying:	***Nɔ bos sɛ yu fayn.***
Translation:	*Do not boast of being pretty, beauty is skin deep.*
Interpretation:	**A person's character is more important than her appearance.**

Parable or Saying:	***Nɔ de mek sɛ yu fayn.***
Translation:	*Do not boast of being beautiful, beauty is from the beholder.*
Interpretation:	**Each person has his/her own opinion about what is beautiful.**

BURDEN, LOAD, PROBLEM OR WEIGHT

Parable or Saying: ***Gɔd nɔ go gi yu lɔd wɛ yu nɔ go ɛbul kɛr.***

Translation: *God will never give you a load that you cannot carry.*

Interpretation: "Come to me, all who are weary and burdened and I will give you rest." (Matthew 11:28). God allows your burden not to tear you down but to build you up. The burden should make you stronger if you trust in the Lord.

Parable or Saying: ***ɛlifant ed nɔto pikin lod.***

Translation: *The elephant's head is no load for a child.*

Interpretation: When you're in trouble, anyway out is a good way out. Take whatever help you can when you are in trouble, even if it has some disadvantages.

CAREFUL, BEWARE, BE CAUTIOUS, THINK TWICE OR WATCH OUT

Parable or Saying: *Fambul tai ná lɛk tik, ĩ kin bɛn, bɔt ĩ nɛba brɔk.*

Translation: *Family tie is like a tree, it bends but never breaks.*

Interpretation: Family members are related for better or for worse. There is no such thing as a broken family.

Parable or Saying: *Fambul tik kin bɛn, bɔt ĩ nɔ de brɔk.*

Translation: *Family tree will bend, but it will not break.*

Interpretation: Family members are related for better or for worse.

Parable or Saying: *Kumbra fɔl nɔ de jomp faya.*

Translation: *Mother hen will not jump over a burning flame while her chicks are by her side.*

Interpretation: Think twice, try to be careful of what you say or do.

Parable or Saying: *Wɛ yu nɔ tinap pan dɔg in tel, ĩ nɔ go bɛt yu.*

Translation: *If you do not step on a dog's tail, he/she will not bite you.*

Interpretation: If you do not upset someone, he/she will not re-act over the whole issue.

Parable or Saying: *Yu padi kin tɔn yu ɛnimi.*

Translation: *A close friend can become your close enemy.*

Interpretation: If there is a close relationship between friends sometimes it may become harmful to the friendship itself. Familiarity breeds contempt!

Parable or Saying: *Nɔ ple wit dɔg tit ɛn uman tɔŋ.*

Translation: *Beware of a dog's tooth and a woman's tongue.*

Interpretation: The teeth are spears and the tongue a sharp sword.

Parable or Saying: *Wɛ yu mek yusɛf lɛk arata, pus go kach yu.*

Translation: *If you behave like a mouse, the cat will catch hold of you.*

Interpretation: If you belittle yourself, people will take advantage of you. Stand up for your rights.

Parable or Saying: *Yu nɔ go put yu tu fut insai watasai fɔ si if ĩ dip*

Translation: *No one tests the depth of a river with both feet.*

Interpretation: Do not throw yourself entirely into a situation if you don't know what is happening. When you are not sure of something or uncertain, you shouldn't jump right into it with everything you have because there is no way back.

Parable or Saying: *Kaw wɛ nɔ gɛt tel, nɔ de rɔnata flai.*

Translation: *A cow that has no tail, should not try to chase away flies.*

Interpretation: God will help or rescue you from any situation.

Parable or Saying: *Kaw nɔ gɛt biznɛs wit ɔs ple.*

Translation: *Cow has no business with horseplay.*

Interpretation: Do not go where you don't belong.

Parable or Saying: *Kakroch nɔ de go usai fɔl dèn de dans.*

Translation: *Roach will not go around the area where rooster/cock and hen are dancing.*

Interpretation: Do not go where you cannot fit in.

Parable or Saying: *Wɛ fish set im mɔt, fishaman nɔ go kach am.*

Translation: *A fish that keeps his mouth shut will not be caught.*

Interpretation: Be careful! Avoid careless talk that will keep the enemy from learning your secrets.

Parable or Saying:	*Di briz wɛ blɔ sotɛ ĩ kɛr mataodo go, nɔto fana ĩ go lɛf biɛn.*
Translation:	*The wind that tosses the mortar away will not spare the winnowing tray.*
Interpretation:	The storms of life that surround the strong also surround the weak.

Parable or Saying:	*Nɔ kɔs di krɔkɔdail tɛ yu dɔn krɔs di watasai.*
Translation:	*Never insult a crocodile until you cross the river.*
Interpretation:	Be careful about criticizing others.

Parable or Saying:	*Krɔs di watasai fɔs, bifo yu go tɔk sɛ di krɔkɔdail gɛt bomp ná ĩ nos.*
Translation:	*Only when you have crossed the river, can you say the crocodile has a lump on his snout.*
Interpretation:	You can't fully know a situation fully unless you've experienced it.

Parable or Saying:	*Krɔs di watasai fɔs, bifo yu kɔs di krɔkɔdail im mami.*
Translation:	*Cross the river before you talk negative about the crocodile's mother.*
Interpretation:	You should take caution and precaution in your actions. "Look before you leap".

Parable or Saying:	*Nɔ bɔn dèm brij wɛ yu waŋ fɔ tek krɔs.*
Translation:	*Don't burn the bridges you need to cross.*
Interpretation:	Do not go ahead and do something knowing you can't step back.

Parable or Saying:	*Flai wɛ de dans frɔnt spaida wɛb go gɛt di spaida in tit.*
Translation:	*A fly that dances carelessly in front of a spider's web, risks the wrath of the spider's teeth.*
Interpretation:	If you fool around with something that is potentially dangerous, you must expect to get hurt.

Parable or Saying:	*Wɛ snek dɔn bɛt yu, wɛ yu si kondo yu go rɔn.*
Translation:	*He who is bitten by a snake fears a lizard.*
Interpretation:	After an unpleasant experience, avoid something similar.

Parable or Saying:	*Wɛ snek dɔn bɛt yu, yu go fred anch.*
Translation:	*He who is bitten by a snake fears an ant.*
Interpretation:	Past experiences can make someone take extra care.

Parable or Saying:	*Wɛ yu de ayd, nɔ lait faya.*
Translation:	*If you are hiding, do not light fire.*
Interpretation:	If you don't want anyone to see you, do not draw attention to yourself by turning on a light or light a fire, it will defeat the purpose of you hiding.

Parable or Saying:	*Wɛ yu ná kɔp andul, yu gɛt fɔ tek tɛm.*
Translation:	*If you are the cup handle, beware of the cup.*
Interpretation:	Work with your spouse as a team and set your family values. Set your boundaries and limits with your in-laws. Be at your best behavior around your in-laws.

Parable or Saying:	*Wɛ yu ple wit shap nɛf, ĩ go kɔt yu.*
Translation:	*If you play with edged tools, you might be slashed.*
Interpretation:	It is dangerous to tamper with mischief or anything that may get you into trouble.

Parable or Saying:	*Yu nɔ go win wɛ yu de trai fɔ rɛsul wit ɔg ná potopoto.*
Translation:	*You will never win if you are trying to wrestle a pig in the mud.*
Interpretation:	Be careful not to argue with an habitual liar, you will get stressed out because he enjoys it and you wll not win. "Wrestle with a pig in the mud. You'll both get dirty; the pig will enjoy it and wins the wrestling match."

Parable or Saying:	*Ná smol anch so kin kil ɛlifant.*
Translation:	*The tiniest ant will kill an elephant.*
Interpretation:	Watch out! Sometimes your worse enemy is much smaller.

Parable or Saying:	*Yu kin was pipul pikin dèm, bɔt nɔ was biɛn dèn yes.*
Translation:	*Bathe other people's children but don't wash behind their ears.*
Interpretation:	Do not be submissive in sweet talking others.

Parable or Saying: *Wɛ blen yai man sɛ lɛ wi stɔn, ĩ dòn tinap pan wan.*

Translation: *If a blind man says let's throw stones, he had stepped on one.*

Interpretation: Think about the consequences before making decisions.

Parable or Saying: *Int no im masta ɛn kabaslɔt no im misses.*

Translation: *Hint knows his master and a long, Creole traditional, female print dress "Princess gown", knows its mistress.*

Interpretation: An action of making something known, especially in an indirect way or an indirect indication or intimation.

Parable or Saying: *Luk bifo yu lip.*

Translation: *Look before you leap.*

Interpretation: Think carefully before any action. Don't jump without looking where you are jumping.

Parable or Saying: *Nɔ tink sɛ krɔkɔdail nɔ de ná di watasai bikɔs di watasai mek yeng!*

Translation: *Don't think there is no crocodile just because the river is calm.*

Interpretation: Be cautious! Do not to rush into a situation or decision before you look into all the possible outcomes. Once you've made that decision, there is no turning back.

Parable or Saying:	*Ekuru dɔg ná in kin kil lɛpɛt.*
Translation:	*A dog with canine scabies; in the face of threats to survive will kill a leopard.*
Interpretation:	Be careful and watchful; make sure to avoid potential danger, mishap or harm.
Parable or Saying:	*Watasai fes fayn, bɔt ĩ denja fɔ slip pan am.*
Translation:	*The face of the river is beautiful, but it is not safe to sleep on it.*
Interpretation:	Don't jump into conclusions to judge a situation without enough information.
Parable or Saying:	*Wet lɛ sɔk lɛpɛt drai, dèn yu go no sɛ di lɛpɛt nɔ to pus.*
Translation:	*Wait patiently until a wet leopard is dried up then you will realize that the leopard is not a cat.*
Interpretation:	Watch-out! Every weakness contains within itself a strength.
Parable or Saying:	*Lili lɛpɛt sɛf ná lɛpɛt.*
Translation:	*Even the smallest leopard is called leopard.*
Interpretation:	Beware! A small person in stature could still be powerful.
Parable or Saying:	*Tek tɛm kil anch, yu go si in gɔt.*
Translation:	*If you take your time to dissect an ant, you will notice his intestines.*
Interpretation:	A careful person achieves his goals by being determined.

Parable or Saying: *Nɔ wɛk dɔg wɛ de slip.*

Translation: *Do not wake up a sleeping dog.*

Interpretation: Don't do anything that will stir up unnecessary trouble.

Parable or Saying: *Lɛ dèm dɔg wɛ di slip lidɔm slip.*

Translation: *Let sleeping dogs lie.*

Interpretation: Be careful! Stay out of the situation if it might cause trouble.

Parable or Saying: *Nɔ dig yu yɔn grev.*

Translation: *Don't dig your own grave.*

Interpretation: Be careful not to be responsible for your downfall.

Parable or Saying: *If yu nɔ tek tɛm wɛ yu de do biznɛs wit pipul, ná dɔg go yit yu sɔpa.*

Translation: *If you are not cautious when you are making your deals you will lose what you have.*

Interpretation: Be alert! Otherwise, you will be responsible for your breakdown.

Parable or Saying: *Wɛ yu waŋ fɔ kɔs dɛf yes man, kɔs am wɛ im pikin de nia yu.*

Translation: *When you want to insult a deaf man, insult him around his child.*

Interpretation: An insecure person, talks negative about another person when the person is not present.

Parable or Saying:	*If yu nɔ kiaful, yu gres go tɔn to gras.*
Translation:	*If you are not careful your Grace will become a bundle of grass.*
Interpretation:	If you are operating in fear and doubt, the door or gate cannot be opened. Fear and doubt is not of God, but of the adversary. You must break free from the adversary's influence to experience His supernatural gifts.

Parable or Saying:	*Fɔ gi lɛpɛt agidi nɔto im ná di tin, ná fɔ kam nia am.*
Translation:	*It is safe to feed a leopard but feeding a leopard at close proximity is dangerous.*
Interpretation:	It is better to expend the time or effort to be cautious with one's actions than to feel regret about one's carelessness later. Be cautious, if you are not, you will regret it.

CERTAIN, ASSURED, CONFIDENT, CONVINCED, POSITIVE OR SURE

Parable or Saying:	*Nɔ kɔnt yu fɔl pikin bifo dèn ach.*
Translation:	*Do not count your chicken before they are hatched.*
Interpretation:	Don't be certain for something that has not yet occurred.

CHARACTER, NATURE, PERSONALITY OR QUALITY

Parable or Saying:	*Wɛ yu tɛl mi udat ná yu kɔna man, á go tɛl yu aw yu tan.*
Translation:	*Tell me whom you love and I'll tell you who you are.*
Interpretation:	If I know who you are dating, I will definitely know your character.

Parable or Saying:	*Yu go sɛ yu pikin fayn pas mi pikin bɔt dèn trik ná di sem.*
Translation:	*You will say that your child is beautiful than my child but all children have sessions of bad behavior.*
Interpretation:	Nobody is perfect and all children will have disruptive behavior. They may have temper tantrums, lie, disobey, argue or talk back to their parents. It may be a clue that something in the child's life needs attention.

Parable or Saying:	*Aw yu mek yusɛf, ná so dèn go bai yu.*
Translation:	The way *someone* acts can help you figure out some key things about *his/her character.*
Interpretation:	A person's way of behaving (good or bad) that is seen and critique by the public.

Parable or Saying:	*Ĩ nɔ sabi fɔ wok wit in an, bɔt ĩ no aw fɔ kɔmpɔt Imsɛf.*
Translation:	*He has no talent but his attitude and outlook make him a great professional.*
Interpretation:	A person who chooses to lead by good example, behaves in a way that shows others how to behave.

Parable or Saying:	*Di lif nɔ fɔdɔm fa frɔm di tik.*
Translation:	*The leaf does not fall far from the tree.*
Interpretation:	Children have the same characteristics as their parents.

Parable or Saying:	*Fawɛ kɔntintri nɔ gɛt chuk chuk.*
Translation:	*Distant cotton tree appears without thorns.*
Interpretation:	When friends are distance apart they usually love and respect their relationships but when living together they tend to find out their bad qualities.

CHARACTER ASSASINATION OR DEFAME

Parable or Saying:	*Wɛ yu pwɛl mi nɛm, yusɛf nɛm go pwɛl.*
Translation:	*If you damage the character of another, you will damage your own.*
Interpretation:	A deliberate and sustained process that aims to destroy the credibility and reputation of a person.

Parable or Saying:	*Ná in nachɔr!*
Translation:	*Your character follows you wherever you go.*
Interpretation:	A person's character is like a shadow. He/she cannot hide from it or run from it. It follows the person for life.

CHEAT, BRIBERY, CORRUPTION, DEFRAUD, DISHONESTY OR SWINDLE

Parable or Saying: *Kɔniman dai, kɔniman bɛr am.*

Translation: *A con-artist buries a con-artist.*

Interpretation: The more cunning a man is, the less he suspects that he will be caught in a simple thing.

Parable or Saying: *Usai smok de, faya de.*

Translation: *Where there is smoke, there is fire.*

Interpretation: The very presence of a rumor means that something is afoot, even if not exactly what is rumored. Rumors always have a grain of truth.

COLD, CHILLY OR COOL

Parable or Saying: *Ĩ kol lɛk dɔg nos.*

Translation: *It is cold like a dog nose.*

Interpretation: It is very cold.

COMPROMISE, AGREEMENT, DEAL, GIVE AND TAKE OR NEGOTIATE

Parable or Saying: *Wɛ yu fɔdɔm ná watasai, yu gɛt fɔ swim ɔ was.*

Translation: *If your fall into a river, you have to swim or take a bath.*

Interpretation: Compromise when you realize that you are not able to stop something.

CONCEAL OR HIDE

Parable or Saying: *Nɔ ayd yu lait ɔnda bushɛl.*

Translation: *Don't hide your light under a bushel.*

Interpretation: If you have special skills or talents, do not conceal them through modesty and prevent others from appreciating or benefiting from them.

CONCERN OR INTERESTS

Parable or Saying: *Tit nɔ de munin.*

Translation: *Even in laughter the heart may be sad.*

Interpretation: Laughter may hide sadness. When happiness is gone, sorrow is always there.

CONFORM OR OBEY THE RULES

Parable or Saying: *Dɔg ná gud polisman, bɔt ĩ nɔ go patrɔl ná di trit wɛ lɛpɛt tap.*

Translation: *Dog is an effective constable but he/she will not patrol in the street where the leopard lives.*

Interpretation: A person should strictly obey rules and not infringe on others' rights.

CONTENTMENT, HAPPINESS OR SATISFACTION

Parable or Saying: *Rop nɔ fit fɔ fɔl nɛk dèn tai am ná im fut.*

Translation: *A rope is not appropriate for the fowl's neck so it is tied on the fowl's foot.*

Interpretation: Things should be placed in the right appropriate position or place.

Parable or Saying: *Apines bɛtɛ pas tait jɛntri.*

Translation: *Being happy is better than being a king.*

Interpretation: Happiness is better than wealth.

Parable or Saying: *Usai dèn tai kaw ná de ĩ fɔ yit gras.*

Translation: *A cow must graze where he/she is tied.*

Interpretation: Be thankful for what you have; you'll end up having more. If you concentrate on what you don't have, you will never, ever have enough.

Parable or Saying: *Wɛ ĩ tap nia watasai, ĩ nɔ go tek pit fɔ was in an.*

Translation: *A person who lives near a river will not use spit to wash his hands.*

Interpretation: Be grateful for what you already have; it is the key to becoming a more fulfilled and satisfied person.

Parable or Saying: *Kaw wɛ nɔ gɛt tel, ná Gɔd de drɛb im flai.*

Translation: *A cow without a tail, God chases his/her flies.*

Interpretation: God will help or rescue you from any situation.

Parable or Saying: *Af brɛd bɛtɛ pas natin ɔ dondo.*

Translation: *A half loaf of bread is better than none.*

Interpretation: Getting only part of what you want is better than not getting anything.

Parable or Saying: *Wan fut bɛtɛ pas tu kane tik.*

Translation: *One foot is better than two crutches.*

Interpretation: Be thankful for what you have, even though it is less than you would like.

Parable or Saying: *Ose tait sotɛ, fɔl de le.*

Translation: *However tightly packed a house might be a hen finds a corner to lay her eggs.*

Interpretation: A person receiving enough attention and love from someone in the same residence or nearby; the lovers become truly silent, relaxed, fulfilled and happy.

Parable or Saying: *Wɛ wan do kloz, anɔda do go opin.*

Translation: *When the door of happiness closes, another one opens.*

Interpretation: An opportunity for development and growth.

Parable or Saying: *Bɔd ná yu an bɛtɛ pas tu bɔd ná bush.*

Translation: *A bird in the hand, is worth two in the bush.*

Interpretation: In short, what you have is better than what you don't have, and it's best not to gamble it away.

Parable or Saying: *Nɔ lɛf di fish wɛ de ná yu an fɔ di fish wɛ de tɔch yu fut.*

Translation: *Do not drop the fish you have in your hand for the fish that touches your foot.*

Interpretation: Stay satisfied with what you have.

CONTROL, AUTHORITY, COMMAND, DIRECT, INSTRUCT, ORDER OR RULE

Parable or Saying: *Gɔd mami fɔ fɔl, tai tumbu ná nɛk fɔ gol chen.*

Translation: *A sponsor for a chicken; wraps a worm around her neck instead of a gold neckless.*

Interpretation: A person with the power to influence or direct people's behavior or the course of events.

CORPORATION, CAUSE & EFFECT, COLLABORATE, GROUP OR PARTICIPANTS

Parable or Saying: *Ná tu pipul kin taŋgo.*

Translation: *It takes two to tango.*

Interpretation: Any situation in which two parties are essential, from romance to fighting.

Parable or Saying: *Ná tu pipul ĩ kin tek fɔ mek plaba ɔ kitikata.*

Translation: *It takes two to quarrel.*

Interpretation: A quarrel is an angry dispute between two persons. An argument or quarrel is never only one person's fault. If the other person refuses to participate then it is not an argument.

Parable or Saying: *Wan an banguls nɔ de shek.*

Translation: *A single bracelet does not jingle.*

Interpretation: There is strength in numbers. It is better to work with a team than to work alone.

Parable or Saying:	*Wan finga nɔ de kach lɔs.*
Translation:	*One finger cannot grab hold of a lice on someone's head.*
Interpretation:	We are like parts of one body; we need to cooperate with each other.

Parable or Saying:	*Ná wan an yu de tek fɔ was de ɔda an.*
Translation:	*You have to take one of your hands to wash the other.*
Interpretation:	People working or acting together for a common purpose.

Parable or Saying:	*Wɛ natin nɔ tɔch di banga tik lif dèm, dèn nɔ go shek.*
Translation:	*If nothing touches the palm-leaves they do not rustle.*
Interpretation:	It is a cause and effect situation. A cause (the wind blowing the palm leaves) and an affect (the palm leaves rustle). What this is saying is, if you don't want something to happen, don't cause it to happen.

COURAGE, AUDACITY, BRAVERY, DARING, GUTS OR NERVE

Parable or Saying:	*Yu nɔ gɛt fɔ krai pan milk wɛ dòn trowɛ ná grɔn.*
Translation:	*You cannot cry over spilt milk*
Interpretation:	To be unhappy about something that cannot be undone.

Parable or Saying:	*ɔmɔs yu go lik pan tɛn pɛns sɔl?*
Translation:	*How much will you taste on ten-penny salt?*
Interpretation:	There is a limit to everything. Doing something once too many can cause disaster.

COURTESY, GOOD MANNERS, NICE OR POLITENESS

Parable or Saying: *Fɔ nais nɔ kɔs dondo ɔ natin.*

Translation: *To be nice costs nothing.*

Interpretation: It doesn't cost a cent to be nice or polite, so why not be nice. You might make someone's day.

Parable or Saying: *Gud tɔŋ ná gud wɛpɔn.*

Translation: *A good tongue is a good weapon.*

Interpretation: We can build up others by the proper and good use of the tongue.

Parable or Saying: *Gud wɔd pul gud kola.*

Translation: *A good word offers the best kola nut.*

Interpretation: Good words enriches someone's mind and soul.

Parable or Saying: *Gud wɔd kin ɔt faya.*

Translation: *A good word extinguishes more than fire.*

Interpretation: Saying nice things to people makes them feel good. People who feel good about themselves are happy and productive.

Parable or Saying: *Gud wɔd nɔ de wes.*

Translation: *A kind word is not wasted.*

Interpretation: A kind word encourages or utters cheers of approval.

COWARD, SCAREDY-CAT OR WEAKLING

Parable or Saying: *Kawad man kin ayd biɛn sɔmbɔdi wɛ ĩ dòn trowɛ ston.*

Translation: *A coward always hides behind someone else after he has thrown a stone.*

Interpretation: Someone who lacks courage and runs the other direction after seeing a person who needs help.

Parable or Saying: *Pus nɔ de krai usai dèn wap am.*

Translation: *A cat never cries where it is stroked.*

Interpretation: A person who is shamefully unable to control fear and literally shrinks from danger or trouble.

Parable or Saying: *Kakroch nɔ gɛt powa ná fɔl kɔntri.*

Translation: *A roach does not have the authority to do anything where there are roosters/cocks and hens.*

Interpretation: A person who is weak physically.

CRIME, CORRUPTION, LAWBREAKING OR WRONG DOING

Parable or Saying: *Dɔg kin kam bak usai ĩ dòn vɔmit.*

Translation: *A dog always returns to his vomit.*

Interpretation: A fool repeats his foolishness.

CRITICIZE, CONDEMN OR PASS
JUDGEMENT ON SOMEONE

Parable or Saying: *Pipul wɛ de ná glas ose nɔ fɔ trowɛ ton-ton.*

Translation: *People who live in glass houses should not throw stones.*

Interpretation: Don't criticize other people if you're not perfect yourself.

Parable or Saying: *Nɔ poynt yu finga wɛ yu gɛt sten glas ose.*

Translation: *Do not point fingers when you have stained glass windows in your house.*

Interpretation: Take a deep hard look at yourself before criticizing others.

Parable or Saying: *Sɛ di krɔkɔdail gɛt bɔmp ná im bak wɛ yu krɔs di watasai.*

Translation: *Say the crocodile has bump on its back before you cross the river.*

Interpretation: If you are vulnerable you should not attack anyone.

Parable or Saying: *Wɛ yu trai fɔ klin ɔda pipul lɛk sop, yu go dai pan wɛtin yu de du.*

Translation: *If you try to clean others like soap, you will waste away in the process.*

Interpretation: Try as hard as you may, you cannot cleanse anyone who wants to keep his dirt. The best help you can give is to point the person to the soap and the water and show him how to clean himself.

Parable or Saying: *Wɛ di fɔks nɔ gɛt di grep ĩ sɛ ĩ sawa.*

Translation: *When the fox can't get the grape, he/she says it sour.*

Interpretation: A low self-esteem person is reinforced by negative talks.

Parable or Saying: *Begaman nɔ gɛt cɔis.*

Translation: *Beggars can't be choosers.*

Interpretation: One should not criticize something that one gets for free.

Parable or Saying: *Lɛ di pɔt nɔ kɔl di tikitul blak.*

Translation: *Pot calls the kettle black.*

Interpretation: Someone criticizes another person for a fault which he/she has himself.

Parable or Saying: *Lɛ ogiri nɔ kɔs kenda sɛ ĩ smɛl.*

Translation: *Let not the fermented sesame seeds insults the fermented locust seeds for its odor.*

Interpretation: Criticizing others for the very fault he/she possesses.

Parable or Saying: *Bol nɔ fɔ laf wɛ kalbas brɔk.*

Translation: *A bowl should not laugh when a calabash breaks.*

Interpretation When someone conceals his/her own faults while seeing the faults of others.

Parable or Saying: *Kamel nɔ de luk ĩ yon bɔmp wɛ ĩ gɛt ná in bak.*

Translation: *A camel never sees its own hump.*

Interpretation: Someone who is always finding faults on others.

Parable or Saying: *Kamel nɔba si aw ĩ nɛk bɛn.*

Translation: *A camel never sees the crookedness of his/her neck.*

Interpretation: Someone who readily finds faults in other people but cannot find his/her own faults.

Parable or Saying: *Nɔ trai fɔ fiks yu nɛba fɛnch bifo yu go ckɛk yu yon.*

Translation: *Do not mend your neighbor's fence before checking on yours.*

Interpretation: Your life will improve when you avoid downgrading your neighbor.

Parable or Saying: *Nɔ kɔl di bush wɛ kɔba yu jɔngul.*

Translation: *Do not call the forest that shelters you a jungle.*

Interpretation: Do not insult someone who is taking care of you.

Parable or Saying: *Wɛ yu nɔ ɛbul dans, yu sɛ di yad gɛt ton-ton.*

Translation: *He who is unable to dance says that the yard is stony.*

Interpretation: Do not make excuses for your failures.

Parable or Saying: *Wɛ yu nɔ sabi dans, yu sɛ dɛn nɔ de bit di bata fayn.*

Translation: *He who cannot dance will say the beat of the drum is awful.*

Interpretation A person expressing strong disapproval of something.

Parable or Saying: *Mɔŋki nɔ de si in yon biɛn, bɔt ĩ de si in kompin yon.*

Translation: *A monkey does not see his own hind part, he sees his neighbor.*

Interpretation: A person finding and pointing out faults or problems.

Parable or Saying:	*Mɔŋki no de si in yon tel, bɔt ī de si in kɔmpin yon.*
Translation:	*A monkey does not recognize his own tail, he sees his neighbor.*
Interpretation:	**People who never recognize their own faults.**

Parable or Saying:	*Mɔŋki nɔba tink sɛ in pikin wɔwɔ.*
Translation:	*A monkey never thinks that her child is ugly.*
Interpretation	**People never see their own faults.**

Parable or Saying:	*Babu de laf in kompin biɛn.*
Translation:	*A baboon laughs at the buttocks of another baboon.*
Interpretation	**A person who indicates the faults of someone and fails to see his own faults.**

Parable or Saying:	*Wɛ yu de poynt wan finga pan sɔmbɔdi, tri finga de poynt pan yu bak.*
Translation:	*If you have one finger pointing at somebody, you will have three pointing towards you.*
Interpretation:	**Stop blaming others and help yourself or look in the mirror, you might just be talking about yourself.**

Parable or Saying:	*Bifo yu tek di dɔti pan yu kɔmpin yai, tek di dɔti ná yu yon yai fɔs.*
Translation:	*Before you remove dirt from one's eyes, remove the one in your eye first.*
Interpretation:	**Confront your own faults, even if you think you are only one percent wrong and the other person is ninety-nine percent wrong.**

Parable or Saying:	*Luk ná glas ɛn si yusɛf, bifo yu poynt yu finga.*
Translation:	*Glance at the image on the mirror before pointing fingers.*
Interpretation:	Look in the mirror, you might just be talking about yourself. 'We want to relocate the ugliness we feel about ourselves and put it into someone else. We say those bad feelings do not apply to us; they apply to someone else'.
Parable or Saying:	*Mɔdènlɔ nɔ mɛmba sɛ in sɛf ná bin dɔtɛnlɔ.*
Translation:	*The mother-in-law does not remember that she was a daughter-in-law.*
Interpretation:	To talk about the problems or faults of someone or something.
Parable or Saying:	*Kaw wɛ ol, tink sɛ im nɔto bin pikin kaw.*
Translation:	*The old cow thinks she was never a calf.*
Interpretation:	To look at and make judgments about someone or something.
Parable or Saying:	*Bifo yu mɛn ɔda pipul, mɛn yusɛf fɔs.*
Translation:	*Before healing others, please heal thyself.*
Interpretation:	Attend to one's own defects rather than criticizing defects in others.

CRY, SOB OR WEEP

Parable or Saying:	*Yu to crai bɛlɛ.*
Translation:	*You cry and whine for everything.*
Interpretation:	A person who sometimes cries, complains or protests in a childish or annoying fashion.

CURIOSITY, INQUISITIVENESS OR NOSINESS

Parable or Saying: *Bizabɔdi ɛn lai.*

Translation: *Curiosity kills the cat.*

Interpretation: Being too nosy or curious may get a person into trouble.

DANGER, JEOPARDY OR RISK

Parable or Saying: *Pikin wɛ nɔ de yɛri wɔd, go si am.*

Translation: *A child who is fearless and does not listen, is going to bring tears to his mother's eyes.*

Interpretation: Children who do not heed their parents' advice will suffer harsh consequences.

Parable or Saying: *Kakroch nɔ gɛt biznɛs pan fɔl fɛt.*

Translation: *Cockroach does not have any business to be around where fowls are fighting.*

Interpretation: Don't meddle in things that don't concern you.

Parable or Saying: *Wɛ flai de dans kiales bifo spaida wɛb, ĩ go gɛt di spaida in tit.*

Translation: *A fly that dances carelessly in front of a spider's web, risks the wrath of the spider's teeth*

Interpretation: Someone not giving sufficient attention or thought to avoid harm or injury.

Parable or Saying: *Flai nɔ gɛt biznɛs fɔ dans bifo kondo.*

Translation: *A fly has no business dancing in front of a lizard.*

Interpretation: Do not go where you don't belong.

Parable or Saying: *Bɔd wɛ gɛt faya ná in tel, go bɔn usai ĩ tap.*

Translation: *A bird with fire on its tail burns its own nest.*

Interpretation: A dangerous person will likely to cause harm or injury to himself or someone else.

Parable or Saying: *Bɔd wɛ pre fɔ ren, go fɛn ĩmsɛf sok.*

Translation: *A bird that prays for rain will find itself soaked.*

Interpretation: A person receives the desires of his/her heart.

Parable or Saying: *Wɛ yu nɔ tinap ná dɔg ĩ tel, ĩ nɔ go bɛt yu.*

Translation: *Do not step on the dog's tail and it will not bite you.*

Interpretation: Avoid an unpleasant situation to prevent it from happening.

Parable or Saying: *Yu nɔ go kik dɔg wɛ de slip.*

Translation: *Don't kick a sleeping dog.*

Interpretation Avoid taking risks.

Parable or Saying: *Wɛ dɔg de bak nɔto powa ĩ de mek, sɔntɛmde ĩ kin de frɛd.*

Translation: *The dog's bark is not might, but fright.*

Interpretation: A person talking or shouting at the top of his/her voice is sometimes indicating fear or simply trying to get you to pay some attention to him.

Parable or Saying: *Dɔg nɔ go yit bon wɛ tai pan snek.*

Translation: *A dog cannot eat a bone tied to a snake.*

Interpretation: Avoid taking risks or danger.

Parable or Saying:	*Wɛ ɔkpɔlɔ tai raun yu fut, luk fɔ snek.*
Translation:	*When a frog is tied around your foot; expect a snake.*
Interpretation:	Avoid a situation involving exposure to danger.

Parable or Saying:	*Nɔ fet layon if yu nɔ to layon.*
Translation:	*Do not try to fight a lion if you are not one yourself.*
Interpretation:	Take precautions in advance to danger.

Parable or Saying:	*Eg nɔ gɛt ɛni bisnɛz fɔ dans wit ston.*
Translation:	*Eggs have no business dancing with stones.*
Interpretation:	Stay away from a situation that will involve exposure to danger.

Parable or Saying:	*Arata nɔ de dans ná pus ĩ dɔmɔt.*
Translation:	*Rat does not dance in front of the cat's doorway.*
Interpretation:	Avoid taking the chances.

Parable or Saying:	*Nɔ waka usai layon de waka.*
Translation:	*Do not walk through the lion's path.*
Interpretation:	Keep away from threat.

Parable or Saying:	*Wɛ kakroch waŋ alaki, ĩ fɛn insɛf ná pamayn bɔtul.*
Translation:	*A cockroach that crawls carelessly into a palm oil bottle; risks its life.*
Interpretation:	A careless and dangerous person will always find himself in danger.

Parable or Saying: *Wɛ kakroch sɛ ĩ waŋ fɔ dans, kɔl man-kak, lɛ ĩ bit di bata.*

Translation: *When cockroach says he wants to dance, call the cock or rooster, have him come and beat the drum for him.*

Interpretation: Stay away from horrible situation to prevent it from happening.

Parable or Saying: *Nɔ kɔs krɔkɔdail tɛ yu dɔn krɔs di watasai.*

Translation: *Never insult a crocodile until you cross the river.*

Interpretation: Avoid the risks! Wait until you get what you need from a person, before you start to abuse him/her.

Parable or Saying: *Nɔ waka go insai snek ol wɛ yu set yu yai.*

Translation: *Do not walk into a snake pit with your eyes closed.*

Interpretation: An irresponsible or careless person who does what he/she likes and does not care what happens afterward.

Parable or Saying: *Kaw nɔ gɛt biznɛs wit ɔs ple.*

Translation: *Cow has no business with horseplay.*

Interpretation: Avoid danger. Do not go where you don't belong.

Parable or Saying: *Nɔ tink sɛ krɔkɔdail nɔ de ná di watasai bikɔs di watasai mek yeng!*

Translation: *Don't think there is no crocodile just because the river is calm.*

Interpretation: Be cautious! Do not rush into a situation or decision before you look into all the possible outcomes. Once you've made that decision, there is no turning back.

Parable or Saying:	*Snek pan yu fut, tik ná yu an!*
Translation:	*Snake at your feet, a stick at your hand!*
Interpretation:	There is a possibility that something harmful or unpleasant will happen.

Parable or Saying:	*Fɔl nɔ go lɛ kakroch fɔdɔm ná ĩ eria.*
Translation:	*A fowl will not spare a cockroach that falls into its path.*
Interpretation:	A careless person who does what he/she likes and does not care what happens afterward.

Parable or Saying:	*Tɛl kakroch fɔ go kɔl fɔl.*
Translation:	*Instruct a cockroach to summon a fowl.*
Interpretation:	You are looking for trouble.

Parable or Saying:	*Ĩ kɔmɔt ná frai pan ɛn go ná faya.*
Translation:	*Out of the frying pan and into the fire.*
Interpretation:	To escape from a bad situation to the worse condition.

Parable or Saying:	*Wɛ yu ple wit faya, ĩ go bɔn yu.*
Translation:	*If you play with fire you will get burned.*
Interpretation:	If you fool around with something that is potentially dangerous, you must expect to get injured.

Parable or Saying:	*Faya nɔ gɛt brɔda ɔ sista.*
Translation:	*Fire does not have brother or sister.*
Interpretation:	Stay out of danger.

Parable or Saying:	*Wε yu si ɔkpɔlɔ de jomp santεm, snek de rɔnata am.*
Translation:	*When a frog continues to hop in the afternoon, it is chased by a snake.*
Interpretation:	An unusual cause is usually responsible for an unusual incidence. Be careful! There might be trouble in the forefront.

Parable or Saying:	*Wε lεpεt kɔmɔt, dèn de yit im pikin.*
Translation:	*When a leopard is away, his cubs are eaten.*
Interpretation:	When a person in authority is away, his friends or relatives are the most threat to those under the person's rule.

DEATH, BEREAVE OR PASSING

Parable or Saying:	*Dai nɔ di tεl yu wε ĩ de kam.*
Translation:	*Death does not sound a trumpet.*
Interpretation:	Get ready. It comes at any time or unexpectedly.

Parable or Saying:	*Dai ná wε ov laif.*
Translation:	*Death is a part of Life. No one escapes its clutches.*
Interpretation:	Death is a natural part of life and yet it is the destination we all share.

DECEIVE, BETRAY, CHEAT, DISHONEST, MISLEAD OR TRICK,

Parable or Saying:	*Skul masta ná bin skul boi.*
Translation:	*A school master was once a school boy.*
Interpretation	A behavior that is meant to fool or trick someone.

Parable or Saying:	*ɛvribɔdi padi nɔ to nobɔdi padi.*
Translation:	*A friend to everybody is a friend to nobody.*
Interpretation:	It isn't possible to be a friend to all because everyone is different, and has different opinions, if you're a friend to all you're two-faced and therefore you are not really a friend to anyone.

Parable or Saying:	*Fisha-man ɔ fisha-uman nɔ go sɛ im fish stink ɔ rɔtin.*
Translation:	*A fisherman or fisherwoman will not say his fish stink or rotten.*
Interpretation:	A person will never talk bad about his family or self.

Parable or Saying:	*Trik ná smok.*
Translation:	*Trick is smoke.*
Interpretation:	A person repeatedly using cunning or skillful act or scheme, intended to deceive or outwit someone.

Parable or Saying:	*Yu ná grin snek ná grin gras.*
Translation:	*He is a green snake in a green grass.*
Interpretation:	A treacherous, deceitful, double-crossing or two-faced person who pretends to support you but secretly tries to harm you.

DECENCY, COURTESY, DIGNITY, HONOR, INTEGRITY. MODESTY OR RESPECT

Parable or Saying: *Tɔn bak to yu ɔl man, nɔ to bambɔt wans yu du am wit disɛnsi.*

Translation: *Dating your ex-lover is not unethical as long as you approach it with caution.*

Interpretation: Love can be rekindled, but it is different the second time around. Let the intimacy grow in the relationship just as it would if it were a new relationship. Take your time getting to know one another again.

DESIRE, CRAVING, LONGING, NEED OR WANT

Parable or Saying: *Wɛ yu nɔ de, á de mɛmba yu.*

Translation: *Absence makes the heart grow fonder.*

Interpretation: The lack of something increases the desire for it.

DESTINE, PREDESTINE OR PREDETERMINE

Parable or Saying: *Wata wɛ ná fɔ yu, ĩ nɔ go rɔn pas yu.*

Translation: *The stream will route to your destination if you are destined for great things.*

Interpretation: What is yours will always be yours. God has given you your destiny before you were born and only you will receive it.

Parable or Saying:	*Wɛtin yu du ɛn aw yu du am, ná im yu go gɛt.*
Translation:	*Whatever you do and how it is done, you will receive the reward.*
Interpretation:	Destiny comes from God but you can miss God's purpose for your life by your own choices.

Parable or Saying:	*Wɛtin Gɔd dòn plant, yu nɔ gɛt fɔ wata am.*
Translation:	*What God has planted to grow is final.*
Interpretation:	God has a plan that he wants you to fulfill and that's your destiny. You can't change your destiny, then why even try?

Parable or Saying:	*Wɛtin Gɔd dòn mak fɔ yu, nɔbɔdi nɔ go tek am from you.*
Translation:	*What is meant to be yours, not a single person will take it from you.*
Interpretation:	As long you stay in obedience to God, when the time is right, you will receive your blessing.

Parable or Saying:	*Wɛtin Gɔd plant ɛn wɛtin mɔtal man plant nɔto di sem.*
Translation:	*What God had planted and that's his will. It is totally different from human being's will.*
Interpretation:	A person's destiny is entirely controlled by God. God's will is automatic. He allows everyone to make choices. If you choose God's will, even when you mess up God can turn disaster into destiny.

Parable or Saying:	*Yu go gɛt wɛtin ná fɔ yu.*
Translation:	*Each man meets his own destiny.*
Interpretation:	A person's destiny is completely determined.

Parable or Saying:	*Go ɔp kam dòn, wɛtin dòn mak fɔ yu, yu go mɔs gɛt am.*
Translation:	*Now or later, you will receive the best of life.*
Interpretation:	If you are destined, you will receive the reward.

DIFFER, CONFLICT OR DISAGREE

Parable or Saying:	*Mi ɛn mi brɔda nɔ gri fɔ natin.*
Translation:	*Children of the same mother do not always see eye to eye.*
Interpretation:	Two individuals who do not agree on something or who do not view something the same way.

Parable or Saying:	*Mi ɛn dèm nɔ gri fɔ natin.*
Translation:	*We can't see eye to eye.*
Interpretation:	People who do not agree on something or do not have similar viewpoint on issues.

Parable or Saying:	*Big fut man nɔ de joyn smɔl fut dans.*
Translation:	*A big foot man does not join a small foot dance.*
Interpretation:	Someone whose point of view is differ from others.

Parable or Saying:	*Ĩ sɛ pɔŋkin nɔto sup, bɔt á sɛ pɔŋkin ná sup.*
Translation:	*Pumpkin is not a tasty soup but in some cases, pumpkin is a tasty soup.*
Interpretation:	A person who sees things differently from his contemporaries in ethical matters.

Parable or Saying: *Kasada gɛt di sem skin bɔt nɔto ɔl tes di sem.*

Translation: *Cassava tubers have the same skin but not all taste the same.*

Interpretation: Two folks who look very much alike but do not possess the same characteristics.

Parable or Saying: *Snek ɛn krab nɔ di slip ná di sem ol.*

Translation: *A snake and a crab do not sleep in the same hole.*

Interpretation: Two people with totally different views might harm themselves. Avoid danger.

Parable or Saying: *Faya ɛn gɔnpawda nɔ di slip togɛda.*

Translation: *Fire and gunpowder do not sleep together.*

Interpretation: Two humans who see situations from many different angles.

Parable or Saying: *Tu watasai wɛ di rɔn di sem we nɔ di yɛri dèmsɛf.*

Translation: *Two waterfalls run the same direction but do not hear each other.*

Interpretation: Two individuals very much alike, but think differently.

Parable or Saying: *Nɔ to ɔl mɔŋki de klem di sem tik.*

Translation: *All monkeys do not climb on the same tree.*

Interpretation: What one person wants to accomplish might be different than what the other person wants.

Parable or Saying: *ɛvri do gɛt ĩ yon ki.*

Translation: *Every door has its own key.*

Interpretation: Each individual puts his or her own interests foremost. Everyone is for him/herself.

Parable or Saying: *Spaida ɛn kondo nɔ di si wan ples.*

Translation: *The spider and the lizard do not see eye to eye.*

Interpretation: Two persons with totally different views; might harm themselves. Avoid danger.

Parable or Saying: *Tu loŋ nos man nɔ de kis.*

Translation: *Two long nose individuals do not kiss.*

Interpretation: Two individuals very much alike, but with different characteristics.

Parable or Saying: *Da tin wɛ de du fɔl nɔto in de du ak.*

Translation: *What a modest chicken confronts in life is different from what an aggressive hawk encounters.*

Interpretation: Two folks who are unlike in nature with different ways. 'Different strokes for different folks'.

Parable or Saying: *Tu bosman nɔ go waka go fa.*

Translation: *Two great talkers will not travel together very far.*

Interpretation: Two individuals who have little to do but talk excessively, do not accomplish anything because of different views.

DIFFICULT, CHALLENGING, COMPLEX, HARD, PROBLEMATICAL OR TOUGH

Parable or Saying: *Tidɛ ná fɔ mi, tumara ná fɔ yu.*

Translation: *Today is mine, tomorrow is yours.*

Interpretation: We take turns being hit by the difficulties (or the pleasures) of life.

Parable or Saying:	*Wɔd ná mɔt nɔto lod ná ed.*
Translation:	*The word from your mouth is not the same as carrying a stack on the head.*
Interpretation:	When something said seems like a good idea but it is difficult to do. Easier said than done.

DISADVANTAGE, TROUBLE OR UNFAIRNESS

Parable or Saying:	*Jakas sɛ dis wɔl nɔ lɛvul.*
Translation:	*Jackass says that this world is not level.*
Interpretation:	Advantage and privilege are both part of life.

DISLIKE, DETEST OR HATE

Parable or Saying:	*Wɛtin wan pɔsin trowɛ ná im ɔda pɔsin waŋt.*
Translation:	*What one person may think is worthless, may be cherished by another person.*
Interpretation:	One man's junk is another man's treasure.

Parable or Saying:	*Wɛtin wan pɔsin lɛk ná pɔizin to ɔda pɔsin.*
Translation:	*What is of great value to one person, may in fact be of no value to another person.*
Interpretation:	One man's meat is another man's poison.

Parable or Saying:	*Wɛ yu luk bɔtɔm kɔntri pot, yu nɔ go drink wata.*
Translation:	*If you look at the bottom of an earthware pot, you'll stop to drink water from it.*
Interpretation:	Despite the obstacles in your way, If you focus, you will achieve the goals that you determined to accomplish.

Parable or Saying:	*Dɔg wɛ yu nɔ de fid, nɔ go gɛt yu tɛm.*
Translation:	*A dog that you do not feed will never heed your call.*
Interpretation:	A person who is not loving or compassionate to others, sometimes he/she will be treated without respect.

Parable or Saying:	*Ná aw yu mek yusɛf dèn go kɔl yu fɔ tɔn fufu ná awujoh.*
Translation:	*It is how you conduct yourself that you will be selected to prepare a pot of African cassava paste, "fufu" during an African feast known as, "Awujoh".*
Interpretation:	Developing a strong sense of self-respect can help you fulfill your potential, develop healthy relationships, and make everyone around you, see you as a person who is worthy of respect. 'If you respect yourself, others will respect you'.

DISOBEDIENT, DEFIANT, NAUGHTY
OR REBELLIOUS

Parable or Saying:	*Pikin wɛ sɛ in mami nɔ go slip insɛf nɔ go slip.*
Translation:	*A child who says that his mother will not sleep, he/she won't sleep either.*
Interpretation:	When a child crosses the line from respectful resistance to abusive or inappropriate defiance, his/her mother has to respond authoritatively to correct that child.

DISRESPECT, BELITTLE, BOLDNESS, IMPUDENCE OR INSULT

Parable or Saying: *Pikin wɛ trai fɔ wɛr im papa in trɔsis go kɔntiniu fɔ fiks di wes wit rop.*

Translation: *A child who tries to wear his father's pants will continue to adjust the waist line with a string.*

Interpretation: If you disrespect your superior, you will be humiliated.

Parable or Saying: *Wɛ yu mek yusɛf lɛk mata ná dɔmɔt, dèn go wep dèn fut pan yu.*

Translation: *If you make yourself into a doormat, people will wipe their feet on you.*

Interpretation: You teach people how to treat you by the way you treat yourself. If you have self-respect for yourself, people will respect you.

Parable or Saying: *Mi ná Shalat, á nɔ no yai.*

Translation: *My name is Charlotte. I do not mind evil eye contact from people. I will still concentrate on my approach.*

Interpretation: A person who is exhibiting lack of respect. A rude, impolite and discourteous person.

Parable or Saying: *Engɛl nɔ de fityai Gɔd.*

Translation: *An angel does not disrespect God.*

Interpretation: If you disrespect your superior, you will be embarrassed.

Parable or Saying: *Yu mɔt shap lɛk sɔd.*

Translation: *The words from her mouth are sharper than a sword.*

Interpretation: Disrespectful words that flow out of our mouth are an indication of the true condition of our heart. Our lives are fed and framed by the words that come out of our mouths. Words can bring life or death into any circumstance, problem or challenge in life.

Parable or Saying: *If yu mɔt tɔn to nɛf, ī go kɔt yu lip*

Translation: *If your mouth turns into a knife, it will cut off your lip.*

Interpretation: Talking too much is downright disrespectful and it will make your life more complicated.

Parable or Saying: *Di pamtri wɛ waŋ fityai san ná brumtik go lɛf ná in ed.*

Translation: *The palm tree that wants to disrespect the sun will be bared with broom sticks.*

Interpretation: If you disrespect your superior, you will be humiliated.

Parable or Saying: *Dɔg nɔ no im mami man.*

Translation: *A female dog who does not mind to have an affair with her mother's husband.*

Interpretation: A person with the capacity to disrespect her own flesh and blood.

Parable or Saying:	*Pikin wɛ waŋ wɛr in dadi in trɔsis ná rop go yit in wes.*
Translation:	*A child who wants to wear his father's pants will have difficulty to choose the right rope to hold up his father's pants.*
Interpretation:	When a child crosses the line from respectful resistance to abusive or inappropriate defiance, his father has to respond authoritatively to correct his child.

DISSIMILAR OR UNLIKE

Parable or Saying:	*Da tin wɛ de du fɔl nɔto in de du ak.*
Translation:	*What a modest chicken confronts in life is different from what an aggressive hawk encounters.*
Interpretation:	Everyone has there on way of doing things or approaching life. 'Different strokes for different folks'.

DISTURB, BOTHER OR INTERRUPT

Parable or Saying:	*Lɛ dèn dɔg wɛ di slip lidɔm de slip.*
Translation:	*Let sleeping dogs lie.*
Interpretation:	Don't do anything that will stir up unnecessary trouble.

EAT, CONSUME OR DEVOUR

Parable or Saying: **Bifo gud yit go wes, ná bɛlɛ go bɔs.**

Translation: *Before good food wastes, allow your stomach to burst open.*

Interpretation: It is better to over eat than to waste delicious food.

Parable or Saying: **Yu yai pas yu bɛlɛ.**

Translation: *Your eyes are bigger than your belly.*

Interpretation: People sometimes over-estimate the capacity of their stomachs.

Parable or Saying: **Nɔ tɔk wɛ yu de yit.**

Translation: *Do not talk while you are eating otherwise, pepper may go down the wrong passage.*

Interpretation: Be attentive when eating.

EMBARRASSMENT, HUMILIATION OR SHAME

Parable or Saying: ***Ná shem á tek fɔ bɛt fatfut.***

Translation: *It takes humiliation to bite a caterpillar.*

Interpretation: The painful emotion resulting from an awareness of having done something degrading and you wish you could disappear from the public's eye.

Parable or Saying: ***Ná shem á de tek fɔ bɛt krab.***

Translation: *It takes embarrassment to bite a crab.*

Interpretation: The painful feeling that arises from the consciousness of something that is improperly done by oneself.

ENEMY, OPPONENT OR RIVAL

Parable or Saying: *Kloz frɛn kin bi yu ɛnimi.*

Translation: *A close friend can become close enemy.*

Interpretation: If there is a close relationship between friends sometimes it may become harmful to the friendship itself. This is because if we are too familiar to some person we will automatically develop a dislike or hate for that person and we have contempt. Even in the case of food we would like to try out different varieties and if not, we would be bored if we eat the same food daily.

Parable or Saying: *Smat ɛnimi bɛtɛ pas dandogo padi.*

Translation: *An intelligent enemy is better than a stupid friend.*

Interpretation: An intelligent enemy will try to avoid any provoking senseless fight, but a foolish friend might possibly get you easily into trouble.

Parable or Saying: *Gud ɛnimi bɛtɛ pas dandogo padi.*

Translation: *A good enemy is better than a stupid friend.*

Interpretation: You can guess what a good enemy is capable of doing and therefore take precautionary measures, escape from danger and win him. In case of a stupid friend, you cannot guess the stupid things that he will do. Sometimes he may put you in great danger.

Parable or Saying: *Nɔ to mi kil yu pus.*

Translation: *I am not the one who put your cat to sleep.*

Interpretation: Someone who actively opposed or strives to be hostile to another person.

Parable or Saying: *Man ɛlɛba ɛnimi ná man.*

Translation: *Man greatest enemy is man.*

Interpretation: A person's greatest enemy is the enemy within, hidden there are dark and destructive emotions, but also hidden there is the light of reason.

Parable or Saying: *Wɛ yu ɛnimi de mek lɛk arata, wack am lɛk layon.*

Translation: *If your enemy is like a mouse, hit him like a lion.*

Interpretation: Your enemy with a quiet manner may often have complicated or dangerous personality. Be vigilant!

ESTABLISH, CONTROL, GAIN OR SECURE

Parable or Saying: *ɔntin man nɔ de fred bush.*

Translation: *A determined hunter is not afraid in the jungle.*

Interpretation: An individual who does not feel fear or anxiety.

EXAGGERATE, OVERSTATE OR OVERSTRESS

Parable or Saying: *Nɔ bigin mek kitikata fɔ natin.*

Translation: *Do not start to quarrel for nothing.*

Interpretation: Don't make a fuss about something that is not important.

EXCLUDE, BE EXCLUSIVE OF OR ELIMINATE

Parable or Saying: *Mi dadi nɔ to butcha, aw yu waŋ mi fɔ no ɔmɔs fɔ ɔg?*

Translation: *My dad is not a butcher, why should I know about the cost of a pig?*

Interpretation: Do not involve me in your incident.

Parable or Saying: *Wɛ Joki banda bin de bɔn á nɔ de. Wɛtin du á fɔ ɔt di faya?*

Translation: *When Joki's vegetable, wooden stall was burning I was not around. How do you expect me to put out the fire?*

Interpretation: Do not involve someone in a certain situation.

EXPERIENCE, KNOWLEDGE OR UNDERSTANDING

Parable or Saying: *Afrikan parɛbul ná lɛk gyal pikin dɛm wɛ ɔ ndastan parɛbul ɛn trai fɔ du di kɔrɛkt tin ná laif.*

Translation: *African parables are like daughters who understand parables and use them to sustain daily lives.*

Interpretation: African parables are African ancestors' treasure of wisdom handed down to their descendants such as; encouragements, warnings, advice on learning, patience, unity, wealth, poverty, community, family, love and marriage. These parables are learned and understood by African descendants to be the best that they can possibly be in the world where they are living.

Parable or Saying: *ɛkpiriens kin tich fulman.*

Translation: *Experience teaches fools.*

Interpretation: You learn more from things that happen to you in real life.

Parable or Saying: *Wɛ yu lan yu go tich.*

Translation: *He who learns teaches.*

Interpretation: He/she patiently learns and teaches someone more about the subject.

Parable or Saying: *Di pruf de ná di pap.*

Translation: *The proof of the pudding is in the eating.*

Interpretation: The real value of a thing can be judge by experience and not from appearance.

Parable or Saying: *Man wɛ no parɛbul in yuz, go sɛtul plaba.*

Translation: *A man who knows the use of proverbs reconciles differences.*

Interpretation: If you can understand the interpretation and lesson behind a proverb, you will understand where your problems begin and how to resolve them.

Parable or Saying: *Bifo bɔd flai, á dòn kɔnt di eg ná in bɛlɛ.*

Interpretation: *Before a bird flies off, I have already counted the eggs in her stomach.*

Interpretation: By the time you are thinking. I have already read your mind and arrived at the solution.

EXTRAVAGANT, OVER THE TOP, SPEND

FOOLISHLY OR WASTEFUL

Parable or Saying: *Nɔ eng yu at pas usai yu nɔ de rich.*

Translation: *Never hang your hat higher than you can reach.*

Interpretation: **Do not spend more than you can afford.**

Parable or Saying: *Kɔt yu kot akɔdin to yu klos.*

Translation: *Cut your coat according to your cloth.*

Interpretation: **Do the best that you can with the money you have and do no more.**

Parable or Saying: *Di pɛni pɛni wɛ yu de kip ná fɔ ɛmiola.*

Translation: *A penny saved is a penny gained.*

Interpretation: **Money that you save is more valuable than money that you spend right away.**

EYES OR EYEBALLS

Parable or Saying: *Wɛ yai nɔ si, at nɔ go pwɛl.*

Translation: *What your eyes do not see, your heart will not grieve.*

Interpretation: **What you don't see does not hurt you.**

FACT, REALITY OR TRUTH

Parable or Saying: *Biznɛs ná biznɛs.*

Translation: *Business is business.*

Interpretation: **The purpose of business is to make profit.**

FAITH, ASSURANCE, BELIEF, CONFIDENCE, RELIANCE OR TRUST

Parable or Saying: *Wɛ wan do kloz, ɔda do go opin.*

Translation: *When the door of happiness closes, another one opens.*

Interpretation: The old door closed and another one opens up to unlimited numbers of new opportunities.

Parable or Saying: *Put yu wahala pan Gɔd. Ĩ de ɔp ná nɛt de wet fɔ yu.*

Translation: *Cast your troubles on the Lord and he will be up all night anyway.*

Interpretation: Cast your cares on the LORD and he will sustain you; he will never let the righteous fall.

Parable or Saying: *Wɛ Gɔd sɛn yu ná ton-ton; ĩ go gi yu tranga sus.*

Translation: *If God sends you on stony paths, HE will give you strong shoes.*

Interpretation: God will provide, if you pray and have faith, trust and obey him.

Parable or Saying: *Gɔd nɔ go gi yu lod wɛ yu nɔ ɛbul fɔ tot.*

Translation: *God will never give you more than you can handle.*

Interpretation: God is faithful, and he will not let you be tempted beyond your ability. He will give you the strength to endure it.

Parable or Saying: *Wɛ yu biliv pan Gɔd, yu nɔ gɛt fɔ wɔri bɔt bi api.*

Translation: *Faith drives out fears, but smiles drives out tears.*

Interpretation: God's love helps to put your fears to rest and smile away your tears.

FALSE FRIEND

Parable or Saying: *Fɔlfes frɛn ná lɛk shado, ĩ go de wit yu wɛ tin bɛtɛ fɔ yu.*

Translation: *A false friend is like a shadow, he will only be with you when the sun is shining.*

Interpretation: A person who only sticks around his/her friend during the prosperous and beneficial moments of life.

FAMILIAR OR ASSOCIATE

Parable or Saying: *Pas yu tap wit di pɔsin bifo yu go no di pɔsin.*

Translation: *Only if you live with a person will you know a person.*

Interpretation: Sometimes appearance can be deceiving. You do not judge a book by its cover.

Parable or Saying: *Ivul pɔsin no usai anɔda ivul pɔsin de slip.*

Translation: *Evil knows where evil sleeps.*

Interpretation: People who have similar characters or similar interests will often choose to spend time together.

Parable or Saying: *Arata no usai ɔda arata dèm de waka.*

Translation: *Rats know the way of other rats.*

Interpretation: Those of similar taste congregate in groups.

Parable or Saying: *Ná di sus sabi usai de pinch.*

Translation: *The shoe knows where the foot pinches.*

Interpretation: No one except the person who is experiencing difficulty knows the source or cause of the obstacle.

Parable or Saying:	*Kam visit mi ɛn kam tap ná tu difrɛn tin.*
Translation:	*Come visit me and come live with me are entirely different.*
Interpretation:	A person that is amusing, interesting and tolerable can often swiftly become less so when his or her feet are permanently lodged under your roof.

Parable or Saying:	*Pipul wɛ tap togɛda kin fityai dèn sɛf sɔmtɛm de.*
Translation:	*Familiarity breeds contempt and distant breeds respect.*
Interpretation:	Close association with someone leads to loss of respect.

Parable or Saying:	*If yu ple wit dɔg ĩ go lik yu mɔt.*
Translation:	*If you continue to play with a dog he will certainly lick your mouth.*
Interpretation:	Familiarity breeds contempt.

FAMILY OR RELATIVE

Parable or Saying:	*Fambul tai ná lɛk tik, ĩ go bɛn bɔt ĩ nɔ go brɔk.*
Translation:	*Family tie is like a tree, it can bend but it cannot break.*
Interpretation:	People are expected to be loyal to one's family or blood relations and as such have greater obligations towards them than to those who do not belong to the family.

Parable or Saying:	*Wɛ yu ná kɔp andul, yu gɛt fɔ tek tɛm.*
Translation:	*If you are the cup handle, beware of the cup.*
Interpretation:	Work with your spouse as a team and set your family values. Set your boundaries and limits with your in-laws. Be at your best behavior around your in-laws.

Parable or Saying:	*Blɔd tik pas wata.*
Translation:	*Blood is thicker than water.*
Interpretation:	Family ties are stronger than other relationships.

Parable or Saying:	*Fambul tik kin bɛn, bɔt ĩ nɔ de brɔk.*
Translation:	*Family tree will bend, but it will not break.*
Interpretation:	Family members are related for better or for worse.

Parable or Saying:	*Fambul go set kitikata bɔt dèn ná fambul.*
Translation:	*Family will quarrel but will still be family.*
Interpretation:	Family members argue, fight and even stop talking to each other at times. But in the end, family is family. The love will always be there.

FAULT, BLUNDER. DEFECT, ERROR OR MISTAKE

Parable or Saying:	*Mɔŋki nɔ de si in yon tel.*
Translation:	*A monkey does not recognize his/her own tail.*
Interpretation:	People never recognize their own faults.

Parable or Saying:	*As di mɔŋki de klem ɔp, ī de sho in tel.*
Translation:	*The higher the monkey climbs the more he shows his tail.*
Interpretation:	People's faults become increasingly obvious as they advance to positions of high office.

FAVOR, GOOD TURN, KINDNESS, PREFERENCE OR SUPPORT

Parable or Saying:	*Lubi nɔto slev ná drɔsup, ná obligeshɔn ĩ de du.*
Translation:	*Rock potash when added in okra soup is owing it a favor to make it thick and slimy.*
Interpretation:	An act of kindness that benefits someone in some way.

Parable or Saying:	*Chariti bigin ná ose.*
Translation:	*Charity begins at home.*
Interpretation:	Be generous to your family before helping others.

Parable or Saying:	*Wɛ yu du gud, gud go fala yu.*
Translation:	*Do good and good will follow.*
Interpretation:	When you help someone or do something useful for others, you will be rewarded.

Parable or Saying:	*Niu brum swip klin bɔt di ol brum no usai di dɔti de ná ɔl di kona.*
Translation:	*A new broom sweeps clean, but an old broom knows every corner.*
Interpretation:	A new leader with a new perspective can easily see where the old leadership missed and then deals with things that have been let go or overseen. However, the old leader knows his/her people and their habits and can easily take care of some situations with finesse because of aged wisdom.

Parable or Saying:	*An go, an kam.*
Translation:	*Reach out your hand and good will follow.*
Interpretation:	When you reach out a hand good things return to you.

Parable or Saying:	*Swip yu ose klin bifo yu swip trit.*
Translation:	*It is better to clean your house than clean the street(s).*
Interpretation:	Take care of your family and people close to you; worry about helping others later.

FEELINGS, VIEWPOINT OR WAY OF THINKING

Parable or Saying:	*Mɔŋki tɔk, Mɔŋki yɛri.*
Translation:	*Monkey speaks; monkey understands.*
Interpretation:	People who think alike understand each other.

Parable or Saying:	*Ná dadi mɔŋki kin mared mami mɔŋki.*
Translation:	*It is Mr. Old-Man Monkey who marries Mrs. Old-Woman Monkey.*
Interpretation:	People who do similar things in life, tend to share the same interests.

Parable or Saying:	*Wɛ insai yu an de krach, ná lɔk.*
Translation:	*When the palm of the hand itches, it signifies the coming of great fortune.*
Interpretation:	If the palm of the hand itches it signifies that money is coming your way.

Parable or Saying:	*Kɔt yu kot akɔdin tu yu klos.*
Translation:	*Cut your coat according to your cloth.*
Interpretation:	Match your actions to your resources, and do not try to live beyond your means.

Parable or Saying:	*Wɛ yu wach pɛni pɛni, di dala go wach dèm sɛf.*
Translation:	*Take care of the pennies and the dollars will take care of themselves.*
Interpretation:	If you take care of little things one at a time, they can add up to big things.

Parable or Saying:	*Wɛ mɔni de tɔk, tru kin sɛ yeng!*
Translation:	*When money speaks, truth stays silent.*
Interpretation:	It's the idea that money brings out the worst in people and makes them lie, cheat and steal to get it, and while money is powerful then the truth is not.

Parable or Saying:	*Yu bɔn wit silva pun ná yu mɔt.*
Translation:	*You were born with a silver spoon in your mouth.*
Interpretation:	You were born into a financially fortunate family.

FIGHT, ARGUMENT, CLASH, CONFLICT, DISPUTE OR QUARREL

Parable or Saying:	*Yɛgɛ yɛgɛ ná mɔt, ná fɔ rak ɛn dòn.*
Translation:	*Heated or angry words are insignificant, let's fight and get it over.*
Interpretation:	A disagreement between two or more people that builds or leads to regrettable words and eventually fist fights.

Parable or Saying:	*Udat di sus fit, mek ĩ wɛr am.*
Translation:	*If the shoe fits you, wear it.*
Interpretation:	Who caused the argument will have to deal with it.

Parable or Saying:	*Plaba go dòn, bɔt wɛtin kɔmɔt ná yu mɔt nɔ go dai.*
Translation:	*Quarrels end but words once spoken never die.*
Interpretation:	Be cautious of your words when you are in a bad mood. You will have many opportunities to change your mood but negative words spoken will always be remembered.

Parable or Saying:	*Ná bad wokman de mek plaba wit in tul.*
Translation:	*A bad workman always quarrels with his tools.*
Interpretation:	Condemning tools for bad workmanship is an excuse for lack of skills.

FINANCIALLY EMBARRASSED

OR WITHOUT MONEY

Parable or Saying: *Trɔki waŋ bɔks bɔt ĩ an shɔt.*

Translation: *A turtle will love to be a boxer but the turtle's hands are too short to box.*

Interpretation: Someone who is living without money or having debts.

Parable or Saying: *Á nɔ go tek natai fɔ frai ston.*

Translation: *One cannot take nut-oil to deep-fry a stone.*

Interpretation: Many things that seem beyond someones capabilities could actually just be difficult to achieve.

Parable or Saying:	*Ɔl kondo lidɔm wit im bɛlɛ ná grɔn, yu nɔ no uz wan bɛlɛ de at.*
Translation:	*All lizards lay flat thus no one knows the lizard that is suffering from upset stomach.*
Interpretation:	With a good appearance, no one will know your problems or that you are financially embarrassed.

Parable or Saying:	*Nɔ ɛng yu at usai yu an nɔ de rich.*
Translation:	*Do not hang your hat higher that you could reach.*
Interpretation:	Do not spend more than you could afford.

FIX, PATCH-UP OR REPAIR

Parable or Saying:	*Wɛ ĩ nɔ brɔk, nɔ fiks am.*
Translation:	*If it is not broken, don't fix it.*
Interpretation:	If something is not damaged, don't try to repair it.

FOOD, CUISINE OR FOODSTUFF

Parable or Saying:	*Fud wɛ nɔ go kil yu, go mek yu fat.*
Translation:	*Food that is not killing is fattening.*
Interpretation:	If the food looks good, smells good and tastes good then just eat it.

FOOL, BUFFOON, CLOWN, LAUGHINGSTOCK OR SUCKER

Parable or Saying: *Fulman kin kiales aw ĩ de spɛn im mɔni.*

Translation: *A fool will easily part with his money.*

Interpretation: A foolish person usually spends his money carelessly.

Parable or Saying: *Ná fulman go tes watasai wit im tu fut.*

Translation: *Only a fool will test a river with both feet.*

Interpretation: You don't jump into a situation without thinking about it.

Parable or Saying: *Ná fulman go tɔsti fɔ wata wɛ ĩ de ná watasai.*

Translation: *In abundance of water the fool is thirsty.*

Interpretation: Only a fool is not satisfied when he/she has everything to satisfy him/her.

Parable or Saying: *Mɔŋki si, mɔŋki du.*

Translation: *Monkey see, monkey do.*

Interpretation: Foolish people mindlessly copy others.

Parable or Saying: *Wɛ yu de waka wit fulman, yusɛf go tɔn to fulman.*

Translation: *He who walks with fools is a fool.*

Interpretation: Someone who associate him/herself with a person who lacks common sense and does something silly that will eventually be harmful.

FOREVER, CEASELESS OR PERPETUAL

Parable or Saying: *Mi ná watasai ston. Wɛ yu go sotɛ ɛn yu kam bak, yu go mit mi ná di sem ples.*

Translation: *Travel here and travel there; the riverside stone is still in its position.*

Interpretation: Object that is incapable of being moved. Firmly fixed or stationary.

Parable or Saying: *Di ston wɛ di wokman dèm nɔ braskitul, ná im ná di alagba naw ná di kɔna.*

Translation: *The stone that the builders rejected is the very head stone of the corner.*

Interpretation: Someone's family and friends did not recognize him/her as the leader. Later, much later, they realized their mistake and gave him/her his rightful place as the authority.

FORGET, FAIL TO RECALL
OR FAIL TO REMEMBER

Parable or Saying: *Di aks de fɔgɛt; bɔt di tik de mɛmba.*

Translation: *What forgets is the ax, but the tree that has been axed will never forget.*

Interpretation: A person who is unable to remember the occurrence of something that happened.

Parable or Saying:	*Man wɛ shit ɔ kaka nɔ de mɛmba; ná di man wɛ tot am de mɛmba.*
Translation:	*A man who excrete does not remember, but the person who cleans his excrete remembers.*
Interpretation:	Someone who does something bad does not always remember, but the person who it affects remembers all the time.

FORTUNE, LUCK, RICHES OR WEALTH

Parable or Saying:	*Wɛ gud luk kam yu wɛ, gi am chia mek ĩ sidɔm.*
Translation:	*When fortune comes to you, offer her a chair.*
Interpretation:	If you become wealthy overnight, start planning how to keep your fortune.

Parable or Saying:	*Wɛ ĩ ren gud luk, ol yu pan ná yu an.*
Translation:	*If it rains fortune, you must hold your dish.*
Interpretation:	If fortune favors your way, pursue it and be wealthy.

FREEDOM, INDEPENDENCE, LIBERTY OR OPENNESS

Parable or Saying:	*Pɔ bɛtɛ pas tait jɛntri.*
Translation:	*To be poor and free is better than to be wealthy and confined.*
Interpretation:	A poor man who lives an innocent and content life, and using no wrong means to improve his fortunes, is happier and better than the rich man who is hypocritical in his words and deceives others, and has won his wealth by such means, thus proving himself to be a fool, a morally bad man.

Parable or Saying:	*Wɛ pus nɔ de, arata tek chaj.*
Translation:	*When the cat is away the mouse will play.*
Interpretation:	When a person in authority is away, those under the person's rule will enjoy their freedom.

Parable or Saying:	*Wɛ lɛpɛt sok, ná im dɛm animal dɛn go ple nia.*
Translation:	*When a leopard is wet this is the time animals play around.*
Interpretation:	When a person in authority exposes his/her weakness, there is freedom to those under the person's leadership.

Parable or Saying:	*Wɛ di masta nɔ de, ɔkpɔlɔ kam insai ĩ ose.*
Translation:	*When the master is absent, the frogs hop in the house.*
Interpretation:	When a person in authority is away, there is liberty to those under the person's rule.

FRIEND, ACQUAINTANCE OR COMRADE

Parable or Saying:	*Padi ná pɔsin wɛ no ɛvritin bɔt yu, ɛn waŋ fɔ bi yu frɛn.*
Translation:	*A friend is one who knows everything about you and still wants to be a friend.*
Interpretation:	*A person whom one knows and with whom one has a bond of mutual affection.*

Parable or Saying:	*Padi wɛ ɛp yu wɛ tin de mɔna yu, ná im dɛn kɔl padi.*
Translation:	*A friend in need is a friend indeed.*
Interpretation:	A friend who helps you when you really need help is a true friend.

Parable or Saying: *Wɛ yu gɛt tru frɛn dèm, yu jɛntri.*

Translation: *If you have true friends, you are wealthy.*

Interpretation: True friends influence those with whom they associate to rise a little higher and be a little better.

Parable or Saying: *Nɔ trɔs niu padi ɔ ol ɛnimi'*

Translation: *Do not trust a new friend or an old enemy.*

Interpretation: Do not place confidence in man but always trust in God.

Parable or Saying: *Kam waka to mi ɛn kam tap to mi nǎ tu difrɛn tin.*

Translation: *Seeing me and living with me are two different things.*

Interpretation: Meeting people casually does not prepare you for what they will be like in close interaction.

GIVE, DONATE, GRANT, OFFER OR PROVIDE

Parable or Saying: *An go, an kam..*

Translation: *Give, and it will be given to you.*

Interpretation: As you give, so shall you receive.

GLUTTON, FOOD LOVER OR OVEREATER

Parable or Saying: *Bifo gud yit go wes, ná bɛlɛ go bɔs. (Bɛlɛ wapi).*

Translation: *I will rather have an upset stomach than waste a delicious food.*

Interpretation: A person who eats more than necessary. 'It is better to overeat than to waste great food'.

Parable or Saying:	*Bɛlɛ nɔ gɛt lukin glas.*
Translation:	*The tummy does not have a mirror.*
Interpretation:	Many people eat more than what is needed by the body because they don't want to waste food or because they do not want their left overs to be thrown into the gabbage.

GOAL, AMBITION, ASPIRATION, OBJECTIVE, PURPOSE OR TARGET

Parable or Saying:	*Put yams ná faya ɛn tek yai de fɛn nɛf.*
Translation:	*Put yams in the fire while you are looking for knife.*
Interpretation:	Something that we really want, we make immense effort to have it accomplished.

GOOD, EXCELLENT, GOOD QUALITY OR SUPERIOR

Parable or Saying:	*Gud nɛm bɛtɛ pas fayn fes.*
Translation:	*Good name is better than being beautiful.*
Interpretation:	A good reputation is better than a good appearance.

Parable or Saying:	*Gud nɛm bɛtɛ pas tait jɛntri.*
Translation:	*Good name is better than riches.*
Interpretation:	A good reputation is better than being wealthy.

Parable or Saying:	*Gud wɔd ná im de pul gud kɔla.*
Translation:	*Saying encouraging positive words make a huge difference to someone.*
Interpretation:	Good words are like honeycomb, sweet to the soul and healing to the bones.

Parable or Saying:	*Gud nɛm bɛtɛ pas mɔni ná yu pɔkit.*
Translation:	*Good name is better than money in your pocket.*
Interpretation:	Good reputation is better than money in your pocket.

Parable or Saying:	*Wɛ di rod gud, yu kin waka de tu tɛm.*
Translation:	*When a road is good, it is used the second time.*
Interpretation:	Someone who received valued assistance to survive, he/she will certainly ask for help the second time.

Parable or Saying: *Ná aw yu mek yusɛf dèn go kɔl yu fɔ tɔn fufu ná awujoh.*

Translation: *It is how you conduct yourself that you will be selected to prepare a pot of African cassava paste, "fufu" during an African feast known as, "Awujoh".*

Interpretation: Developing a strong sense of self-respect can help you fulfill your potential, develop healthy relationships, and make everyone around you, see you as a person who is worthy of respect. If you respect yourself, others will respect you.

Parable or Saying: *Wɛ yu mek yusɛf gud, pipul go rɛspɛkt yu.*

Translation: *If you conduct yourself with integrity and treat others with dignity, people will respect you.*

Interpretation: Being a good example is most important, it is a part of who and what you are! Respect for self and others, trust, honesty and so on are many reasons to be a good example.

Parable or Saying:	*Gud biginin kin ɛn gud.*
Translation:	*A good beginning makes a good end.*
Interpretation:	If a task is carefully planned, there's a better chance that it will be well accomplished.

Parable or Saying:	*Gud man kin mek gud wɛf.*
Translation:	*A good husband makes a good wife.*
Interpretation:	If a husband treats his wife well, she will treat him well in return. If a husband wants his wife to be respectful and loving to him, he should be respectful and loving to her.

Parable or Saying:	*Ĩ tranga fɔ fɛn gud man.*
Translation:	*A good man is hard to find.*
Interpretation:	It is difficult for a woman to find a suitable partner.

GOOD COOKING, COOKERY, CUISINE OR FOOD PREPARATION

Parable or Saying:	*Man lɛk uman wɛ sabi kuk bad, bad wan.*
Translation:	*Good cooking is a woman's path to a man's heart.*
Interpretation:	A woman wins a man's warmth through her tasty home cooked meals. She fed his stomach and found love in his heart.

Parable or Saying:	*Man lɛk uman wɛ kin kuk dɛn tait sup fɔ am.*
Translation:	*The way to a man's heart is through his stomach.*
Interpretation:	A woman gains a man's affections by preparing him delicious home cooking meals.

GOSSIP, CHATTERING, HEARSAY, INFORMATION, NEWS OR RUMOR

Parable or Saying: *Wɛ Creole uman dèm waŋ fɔ kongosa ná dèn kɔmuniti dèn kin wɛr kabaslɔt ɛn ol kɔtoku.*

Translation: *When Creole women want to spread rumors like wild fire in their community, they wear traditional Creole female gowns "kabaslɔt" and carry traditional Creole drawstring cloth purses "kɔtoku".*

Interpretation: Gossip gives Creole women a feeling of fitting in with others, reduces stress, helps to make friends, helps to deal with everyday life, dissect relationships with other women, helps to share their experiences with other women, makes them feel good about themselves feel guilty and gives them opportunity to network.

Parable or Saying:	*Kongosa!*
Translation:	*Gossip!*
Interpretation:	Idle talk or rumor, especially about the personal or private affairs of others.

Parable or Saying:	*Kongosa ɛn lai.*
Translation:	*Gossip that can be false.*
Interpretation:	When people spread rumors or lies about a person in order to purposely cause pain or damage.

Parable or Saying:	*Dèn gi am kongosa bɛnch.*
Translation:	*They gave her a bamboo gossip bench.*
Interpretation:	The owner of a gossip bench knows everything and anything about everyone around by engaging in idle talk, tittle tattle, usually concerning other people's private and personal affairs.

Parable or Saying:	*Ĩ sidɔm ná kongosa bɛnch.*
Translation:	*She sits on a bamboo gossip bench.*
Interpretation:	A person who sits on a gossip bench, habitually spreads intimate or private rumors or facts of others.

Parable or Saying:	*Nɔto wan pɔsiŋ de kongosa.*
Translation:	*It takes more than one person to gossip.*
Interpretation:	Casual, unconstrained conversation or reports about other people, typically involving details that are not confirmed as being true.

Parable or Saying:	*Yu ná brɔkos.*
Translation:	*You are a gossiper who tries to break up family or friends.*
Interpretation:	Someone who hears the latest news, spread rumors that will break up family or friends.

Parable or Saying:	*Yu mɔt to lait pan pipul dèn tɔk; kongosa.*
Translation:	*Your mouth is too much on the personal affairs of people.*
Interpretation:	Someone who reveals personal information about others or spreads rumors and scandals.

Parable or Saying:	*Kongosa nɔ gɛt fut bɔt ĩ kin travul.*
Translation:	*Bad news has no feet but travels.*
Interpretation:	Unfavorable information becomes known quickly due to the fact that people eagerly transmit bad news in a chain of speakers and listeners.

Parable or Saying:	*Kongosa kin travul kwik.*
Translation:	*Bad news travels fast.*
Interpretation:	Bad news circulates quickly because people are quick to discuss the misfortunes of others.

Parable or Saying:	*Wɛ yu de tɔk bɔt dɛf yes man, tɔk ná im pikin yes.*
Translation:	*When you want to gossip a deaf man, talk about him in the presence of his child.*
Interpretation:	Only a narrow minded or an insecure person talks about someone behind his back what he will not say to the person's face to feel good.

Parable or Saying:	**Wɔd nɔ gɛt wing, bɔt dèn kin flai far.**
Translation:	*Words have no wings but they can fly a thousand miles.*
Interpretation:	When a person lies; obviously the lies need another lie to support them because lies have no legs to support them to stand; but they have wings and can fly, far and wide.

Parable or Saying:	**Udat de kam kongosa to yu, go kongosa yu.**
Translation:	*He/she who gossips to you will also gossip about you.*
Interpretation:	Be careful who you share your secrets with because not everyone is looking out for your best interest. Choose wisely and pay attention, most of the time people will reveal their true intentions.

Parable or Saying:	**Dèn de rid yu sambalɛta.**
Translation:	*They are spreading rumors to damage your good reputation.*
Interpretation:	People spreading false statement to destroy someone's reputation in order to feel good about themselves, and to feel like they have power over others.

Parable or Saying:	**Wɛ yu nɔ yɛri ɛni nuiz, di nuiz gud.**
Translation:	*No news is good news.*
Interpretation:	Not hearing about a situation suggests that nothing bad has happened or not hearing any news signifies that nothing is wrong.

Parable or Saying:	*Wɛtin yu go tɔk oba dai layon bɔdi, yu nɔ go tɔk am wɛ ĩ de laif wan.*
Translation:	*What is said over the dead lion's body, could not be said to him alive.*
Interpretation:	You can say something behind someone's back, but face to face you cannot.

Parable or Saying:	*Wɛ yu waŋ fɔ yɛri wɛ dɛn dɛ kongosa ná yu kɔ muniti, trai fɔ go kloz to yu ɛnimi.*
Translation:	*When you want to hear the necessary information from the community, stay around your enemies.*
Interpretation:	People in a community talking about the personal or private lives of others or talking negative about a subject matter and no one has the facts.

Parable or Saying:	*Usai smok de, faya de.*
Translation:	*Where there is smoke, there is fire.*
Interpretation:	The very presence of a rumor means that something is afoot, even if not exactly what is rumored. If something looks wrong then it probably is wrong.

Parable or Saying:	*Dɔg wɛ brin bɔn, go kɛr bɔn.*
Translation:	*A dog that will fetch a bone will carry a bone.*
Interpretation:	Beware of people who bring you gossip about others, because they are equally likely to pass on gossip about you.

Parable or Saying:	***Dèn de tɔl yu bɛl yu de aks udat dai.***
Translation:	*They made a bad comment about an individual without him/her knowing.*
Interpretation:	**Someone is gossiping you but you have no knowledge of the situation or fact.**

GRATEFUL, APPRECIATIVE OR THANKFUL

Parable or Saying: **Dɔg nɔ de fɔgɛt in masta.**

Translation: *A dog never forgets his/her master.*

Interpretation: A person who feels or shows an appreciation of kindness.

Parable or Saying: **Dɔg go kam bak usai dèm fid am.**

Translation: *A dog returns to where it was fed.*

Interpretation: A person returned to where he was helped and showed appreciation and gratitude.

Parable or Saying: **Wɛ yu fɔdɔm fɔ mi, á go fɔdɔm fɔ yu.**

Translation: *If you fall for me, I will fall for you.*

Interpretation: If you help me, I will help you or if you do me a favor, I will return the favor.

Parable or Saying: *Wɛ sɔmbɔdi du gud fɔ yu, nɔ fɔgɛt.*

Translation: *One good turn deserves another.*

Interpretation: A kindness is properly met with another kindness or when a person had done a helpful or kind act for someone who had done something good to him.

Parable or Saying: *Wɛ di wɛl drai, ná di tɛm wi kin no sɛ wata gud,*

Translation: *When the well dries, we know the worth of water.*

Interpretation: If you take something for granted, you will miss it as soon as it is gone. When you are lacking of something, you know the true value of it.

Parable or Saying: *Yu nɔ go bɛt di finga wɛ de fid yu.*

Translation: *You do not bite the finger that feeds you.*

Interpretation: It is not a good idea to hurt the person that takes care of you.

Parable or Saying: *An go, an kam.*

Translation: *If you stretch out your hand; another hand will be stretched out to you in return.*

Interpretation: When you reach out a hand good things come back to you.

Parable or Saying: *Wɛ watasai de rɔn dɔŋ, ĩ nɔ de fɔgɛt usai ĩ kɔmɔt.*

Translation: *No matter how far a stream flows, it never forgets its source.*

Interpretation: Showing or expressing thanks, especially to another person.

Parable or Saying: *Da watasai wɛ go fɔgɛt usai ĩ kɔmɔt, go drai.*

Translation: *Any river that forgets its source will definitely dried up.*

Interpretation: When you're thankful for what you have, you are always rewarded with more.

Parable or Saying: *Nɔ fɔgɛt di brij wɛ yu krɔs.*

Translation: *Do not forget the bridge that crosses you over.*

Interpretation: Show or express thanks, especially to another person.

Parable or Saying: *Nɔ kɔs di brij wɛ yu krɔs.*

Translation: *Never abuse the bridge that you've crossed.*

Interpretation: Always thank someone because of something that he or she has done for you.

GREED, AVARICE, COVETOUSNESS OR SELFISH

Parable or Saying: *Wɛ yu waŋ fɔ kach tu arata wantɛm, yu nɔ go kach nɔn.*

Translation: *When you want to catch two rats at the same time, you will never catch any.*

Interpretation: Overwhelming urge of having to have more of something, you will lose everything.

Parable or Saying: *Wɛ yu trowɛ tɔn fɔ kach tu bɔd, yu nɔ go kach nɔn.*

Translation: *If you throw stone to catch two birds at the same time, you will never catch any.*

Interpretation: If you have selfish and excessive desire for more of something that is needed, you will lose everything.

Parable or Saying: *If yu waŋt ɛvritin, yu go lɔs ɛvritin.*

Translation: *If you want everything every time, you will lose everything every time.*

Interpretation: Who wants too much, will not get anything or if you want to get too much you will end up by losing everything.

Parable or Saying: *If yu waŋt ɔl, yu go lɔs ɔl.*

Translation: *He who wants all, will lose all.*

Interpretation: Grasp all, lose all.

Parable or Saying: *Wɛ yu briŋ sɔmbɔdi fɔ kam slip ná yu pala, ĩ go wan fɔ slip ná yu rum.*

Translation: *If you invite someone to sleep in your living room, he/she will want to sleep in your room.*

Interpretation: Taking care of your own needs and feelings without the thought for others.

Parable or Saying: *ɔmɔs yu go lik pan tɛn pɛns sɔl?*

Translation: *How much could you nip on ten penny salt?*

Interpretation: The desire to own and control more resources than others.

Parable or Saying: *Yu gridi lɛk pun bak.*

Translation: *You are as greedy as the back of a spoon.*

Interpretation: A person having or showing an intense and selfish desire for something, especially wealth or power.

Parable or Saying:	*Dɔg wit fɔ fut nɔ go waka ná fɔ rɔd waŋ tɛm.*
Translation:	*A dog with four feet never walk on four roads at the same time.*
Interpretation:	Someone who wants more of something than he is entitled to or the behavior of wanting more than you are entitled to.

Parable or Saying:	*Watasai wɛ dòn ful, ĩ go waŋ fɔ ful mɔ.*
Translation:	*A river that is full still wants to full.*
Interpretation:	Having or showing a selfish desire for more than is needed or deserved, especially money, wealth, food, or other possessions.

Parable or Saying:	*Yu yai big pas yu bɛlɛ.*
Translation:	*His eye is bigger than his stomach.*
Interpretation:	Some people sometimes over-estimate the capacity of their stomachs.

Parable or Saying:	*Di fud wɛ swit gɔt mɔt, ná im go rɔn in bɛlɛ.*
Translation:	*What tastes sweet in goat's mouth will later upset his or her stomach.*
Interpretation:	Matters that appear all right now could hurt you later.

GREET, ACKNOWLEDGE, SALUTE OR WELCOME

Greeting:	*Ek'abọ*
Translation:	*Welcome*
Interpretation:	Manner of greeting someone or everyone

Parable or Saying: *Ek'ushe.*

Translation: *Welcome.*

Interpretation: To greet someone in a friendly way or to acknowledge someone for what he/she has done.

Parable or Saying: *Ekaro.*

Translation: *Good morning.*

Interpretation: Expressing good wishes on meeting or parting during the morning.

Parable or Saying: *Ekasan.*

Translation: *Good afternoon.*

Interpretation: Expressing good wishes on meeting or parting during the afternoon.

Parable or Saying: *Ekale.*

Translation: *Good evening.*

Interpretation: Expressing good wishes on meeting or parting during the evening.

Parable or Saying: *Edaro.*

Translation: *Good night.*

Interpretation: Expressing good wishes on parting at night or before going to bed.

Farewell: *Od'abọ.*

Translation: *Goodbye or ta-ta.*

Interpretation: A farewell remark to someone or everyone.

Farewell: Á de tek yai go lɛf yu ná rod.

Translation: *Goodbye or ta-ta.*

Interpretation: A farewell statement to someone.

Farewell:	*Wi de tek yai lɛf unu ná rod.*
Translation:	*Goodbye or ta-ta.*
Interpretation:	A farewell statement to everyone.

GROUP, BAND, COMPANY OR UNITE

Parable or Saying:	*Mɔŋki dèn ná bai pati, pigin dèn ná bai pia.*
Translation:	*Monkeys are by party, pigeons are by pair.*
Interpretation:	People who are a lot alike tend to gather together and become friends.

Parable or Saying:	*Ivul pɔsin no usai anɔda ivul pɔsin de slip.*
Translation:	*Evil knows where evil sleeps.*
Interpretation:	People who have similar personalities or similar interests will often choose to spend time together.

Parable or Saying:	*Bɔd dèm wɛ fiba de togɛda.*
Translation:	*Birds of the same feather flock together.*
Interpretation:	People tend to associate with those of similar character, interests, or opinions; often used with derogatory implications.

Parable or Saying:	*Wɛ yu de ná grup, di layon nɔ go bɛlful.*
Translation:	*As long as you stay in a group, the lion will stay hungry.*
Interpretation:	Unity means oneness, or togetherness. When there is oneness there is likely to be more strength in opinion, more strength in action, and more strength in character.

Parable or Saying:	*Wɛ ɛnimi nɔ de insai yu ose, di ɛnimi ausai nɔ go gɛt yu.*
Translation:	*When there is no enemy within, the enemies outside will not hurt you.*
Interpretation:	If family members work as a team without any traitor; they are invincible.

GUILT, FAULT OR RESPONSIBLE

Parable or Saying:	*Udat gilti kin tɔk bɔku.*
Translation:	*He who is guilty is the one who has much to say.*
Interpretation:	When a person makes an accusation or finger pointing, check to be sure if that person is not the guilty one.

Parable or Saying:	*Trai dis banguls, if ī fit yu wɛr am, bɔt if ī de at you an trowɛ if ivin ī de shayn.*
Translation:	*Try this bracelet, if it fits you wear it, but if it hurts you, throw it away no matter how shiny.*
Interpretation:	If the statement applies to you, admit it or do something about it.

Parable or Saying:	*Trai dis kot; if ī fit wɛr am.*
Translation:	*Try this coat; if it fits you wear it.*
Interpretation:	If a description applies to you, then accept it.

HABIT, CUSTOM, PATTERN,
PRACTICE OR ROUTINE

Parable or Saying: *Mɔŋki nɔ go lɛf im blak an.*

Translation: *A monkey will always have his/her black hands.*

Interpretation: It is impossible to change someone's ways or habits, especially if he is old and resists change.

Parable or Saying: *Kɔmiɛl go chenj in skin kɔla bɔt ĩ nɔ go chenj in skin.*

Translation: *A chameleon alters the shade of its skin to blend into its environment but its real skin remains the same.*

Interpretation: A person who adjusts his behavior or beliefs in order to please others to succeed but the individual still maintains his/her regular manners.

Parable or Saying: *Lɛpɛt nɔ go chenj in spɔt.*

Translation: *A leopard will never change its spots.*

Interpretation: A person's character, especially if it is bad will not change, if even he/she pretends it will.

Parable or Saying:	*Ren bit lɛpɛt skin sotɛ, bɔt ĩ gɛt in spɔt ná im bɔdi.*
Translation:	*Rain washes a leopard's skin, but it does not wash out its spots.*
Interpretation:	In life each person will encounter hardship, which in this proverb is represented by rain. Hardship is temporary and can only strengthen a person in the future.

Parable or Saying:	*Nɛva rɛsul wit ɔg ná pɔtɔpɔtɔ; una tu go dɔti. Ĩ lɛk dat ɛn ĩ go win di fɛt.*
Translation:	*Never wrestle with a pig in the mud; both of you will get dirty. The pig will like it and win the fight.*
Interpretation:	Someone's behavior that is repeated regularly becomes his/her usual habit.

Parable or Saying:	*Wud go de bɔtɔm watasai sotɛ, bɔt ĩ nɔ go tɔn krɔkɔdail.*
Translation:	*A wood will remain forever in the river but will never be a crocodile.*
Interpretation:	A negative behavior pattern that is repeated often; the person is unaware of it and then it becomes habit.

Parable or Saying:	*Tifman ná tifman.*
Translation:	*A thief will always be a thief.*
Interpretation:	Someone's action or pattern of behavior that is repeated so often that it becomes typical of the person.

Parable or Saying:	*Yu nɔ go tich bush rɔd to ol babu.*
Translation:	*You do not teach the path of the forest to an old guerilla.*
Interpretation:	A negative conduct that is reiterated often; the person is unaware of it and then it becomes habit.

Parable or Saying:	*Yu kin pul sɔmbɔdi ná bush, bɔt yu nɔ go tek di bush trik kɔmɔt pan am.*
Translation:	*You can take a man out of a jungle but you cannot take the jungle out of a man.*
Interpretation:	Someone's conduct that is repeated regularly or usually, often without thinking about it because the person had done it so many times.

Parable or Saying:	*Dɔg ná dɔg.*
Translation:	*A dog does not mind being called a dog.*
Interpretation:	A routine that is acquired from repeating similar behaviors. These habits can also be associated to the instinct and heritage.

Parable or Saying:	*Yu nɔ go tich ol dɔg niu trik.*
Translation:	*You do not teach an old dog a new trick.*
Interpretation:	It is impossible to change someone's ways or habits, especially if he/she is old and resists change.

Parable or Saying:	*Wɛtin dɔti boi waŋ fɔ yɛri? "Pɔmp lɔk".*
Translation:	*What does an untidy boy wants to hear? "The tap is closed".*
Interpretation:	An undesirable behavior pattern that is repeated often; the person is unaware of it and then it becomes habit.

Parable or Saying: **Bad abit ná lɛk faya, if yu ple wit am, ī go bɔn yu.**

Translation: *A bad habit is like fire you can't play with it and expect not to get burned.*

Interpretation: A person with habitual behavior considered to be detrimental to someone's physical or mental health and often linked to a lack of self-control.

HANDOUTS, AIDS OR ASSISTANCES

Parable or Saying: **Beg sɔl nɔba kuk sup.**

Translation: *Borrowed salt is never enough to prepare a delicious meal.*

Interpretation: Handouts never solve one's problem.

HAPPINESS, CONTENTMENT OR PLEASURE

Parable or Saying: **Nɔ wɔri, bi api.**

Translation: *Don't worry be happy.*

Interpretation: Do not become anxious about anything; everything will be all right if you try to change the situation by your actions.

Parable or Saying: **Nɔ bi yu wɔs ɛnɛmi.**

Translation: *Where there is no enemy within, the enemy outside cannot hurt you.*

Interpretation: If you are happy with yourself, no one can bring you down.

HARDSHIPS OR THE STORMS OF LIFE

Parable or Saying: *Wata pas flawa.*

Translation: *A cup of water exceeds a bowl of flour.*

Interpretation: Times are hard.

Parable or Saying: **Plasas dòn pas rɛs.**

Translation: *A bowl of palava/palaver sauce exceeds a plate of cooked rice.*

Interpretation: A person surviving difficult times and challenging adversity.

Parable or Saying: *Wɛ yu fɔdɔm; grap, shek di dɔti ná yu klos ɛn trai egen.*

Translation: *When you fall, dust yourself up and try again.*

Interpretation: Sometimes you have to dust yourself up, pick your head up, put a smile and continue going on with your life. No matter how many mistakes you have made, try again to succeed. God has his plans and his future for you. Don't doubt him, he knows what he is doing.

Parable or Saying: *Wɛ yu fɔdɔm; grap kwik bikɔs dèn go mas yu pas.*

Translation: *When you fall, try to be on your feet or else someone will trample on you.*

Interpretation: People will knock you down and try to intimidate you but if you get up and dust yourself off, they will be intimidated.

Parable or Saying: *Nɔ luk usai yu fɔdɔm bɔt luk usai yu slipul.*

Translation: *Do not look where you fell but where you slipped.*

Interpretation: If you make a mistake, look at what caused you to make it and then try not to make the same mistake again.

HEARTLESSNESS, CRUELTY, MEANNESS, RUTHLESSNESS OR SPITEFULNESS

Parable or Saying: *Dis ná laf ná bɛrin.*

Translation: *Laughing your head off during a funeral which is totally inappropriate.*

Interpretation: Thing which is hoped for but is illusory or impossible to achieve. Things that will never occur or happen.

HINT, ALLUDE TO, IMPLY, INSINUATE OR REFER TO

Parable or Saying: *Int no im masta, kabaslɔt no im misis.*

Translation: *Hint knows its master and a long traditional, Creole female African print dress 'kabaslot', knows its misses.*

Interpretation: When someone is making a suggestion in an indirect way or when an individual is insinuating something.

Parable or Saying: *If di sus du fɔ yu, wɛr am.*

Translation: *If the shoe fits you, wear it.*

Interpretation: If this comment pertains to you, then you have to acknowledge it.

Parable or Saying: *If di kiap du fɔ yu, wɛr am.*

Translation: *If the cap fits you, wear it.*

Interpretation: If this remark applies to you, then you must accept it.

HOSPITALITY, GENEROSITY, KINDNESS, WARMTH OR WELCOME

Parable or Saying: *Ose tait sotɛ, fɔl de lay.*

Translation: *However tightly packed a house might be a hen will always find somewhere to lay its eggs.*

Interpretation: Someone who is known for being hospitable to guests, visitors or strangers. This may also mean that he/she is constantly having a full house at Thanksgiving.

HUMILITY, HUMBLE, MEEK OR MODEST

Parable or Saying: *Kaw nɔ to gud fɔ tot in gras.*

Translation: *A cow is not too good to carry his own grass.*

Interpretation: A person who is outwardly humble and at the same time not being weak.

Parable or Saying: *Gud nɛm bɛtɛ pas gol.*

Translation: *A good name is better than gold.*

Interpretation: A good reputation is more desirable than gold.

Parable or Saying:	*Put yai dɔŋ fɔ si yu nos.*
Translation:	*Position your eyes downward so that you will see your nose.*
Interpretation:	A person who wants the best in life should be ready to work hard and be humble.

Parable or Saying:	*ɔkrɔ nɔ ba langa pas ĩ masta.*
Translation:	*Okra tree will never grow taller that the sower.*
Interpretation:	A respectful child receives parental instructions.

Parable or Saying:	*Pikin wɛ sabi was in an go yit wit bigman.*
Translation:	*If a child knows how to wash his or her hands, he/she would eat with kings.*
Interpretation:	A young person having a sense of respect will participate with elders.

Parable or Saying:	*Pikin wɛ sabi was in an go yit wit di alagba dèm.*
Translation:	*If a child knows how to wash his or her hands, he/she would eat with kings.*
Interpretation:	A young person who is disciplined and well-mannered will participate with elders.

HUNGRY, HUNGER OR STARVE

Parable or Saying:	*Wɛ yu nɔ sabi plant, yu go dai wit angri.*
Translation:	*He, who does not cultivate his field, will die of hunger.*
Interpretation:	A person who is unwilling to work or use any effort will starve to death.

Parable or Saying: **_Angri bɛlɛ nɔ de yɛri nɔbɔdi, wɛ ĩ waŋ yit._**

Translation: _A hungry stomach does not hear a word until it is filled._

Interpretation: Someone who concentrates on his/her needs for food and nothing else.

Parable or Saying: **_Angri bɛlɛ nɔ get yes._**

Translation: _Hungry belly has no ears._

Interpretation: An individual who has a strong craving or desire for food and nothing else will satisfy that person.

Parable or Saying: **_ɛmti bag nɔ de tinap._**

Translation: _An empty sack cannot stand up._

Interpretation: You can't get much work done on an empty stomach.

Parable or Saying: **_Angri mɛk mɔŋki champ pɛpɛ._**

Translation: _Hungry made the monkey ate hot pepper._

Interpretation: Necessity or hard times forces people to do strange things.

IDENTITY, SELF OR UNIQUENESS

Parable or Saying: **_Pɔli tɔk sotɛ, ná bɔd._**

Translation: _No matter how a parrot talks, a parrot is still a bird._

Interpretation: "Be yourself" is the best advice you can give to people.

Parable or Saying: **_Yu kin mek babu nos sotɛ, ĩ still wɔwɔ._**

Translation: _No matter how you fix a baboon's nose, he/she is still ugly._

Interpretation: "Be yourself" is the best advice you can give to people

Parable or Saying:	*Wud de bɔtɔm watasai sotɛ ĩ nɔ go tɔn krokodial.*
Translation:	*No matter how long a log stays in the river, it doesn't become a crocodile.*
Interpretation:	"Be original" is the best advice you can give to people.

IDLE, LAZY, SLUGGISH OR WORK-SHY

Parable or Saying:	*Yu klap yu an ɛn yu klap yu fut.*
Translation:	*You fold your hands and feet in a changeless situation.*
Interpretation:	A person spending time doing nothing, lacking responsibility or not having a job.

IGNORANT, BAD MANNERED, BADLY INFORMED, RUDE OR UNAWARE

Parable or Saying:	*Á tot yu, yu nɔ no sɛ rod fa.*
Translation:	*He who is being carried does not realize how far the town is.*
Interpretation:	A person who is not feeling or showing gratitude.

Parable or Saying:	*Dèn de tol yu bɛl yu de aks udat dai.*
Translation:	*The discussion is about you and you are asking, "Who are they talking about?"*
Interpretation:	A person not having enough knowledge, understanding, or information about something.

Parable or Saying:	*Ignɔrant ná kɔs.*
Translation:	*Ignorant is a cuss or curse.*
Interpretation:	With more knowledge, a person tend to have a better chance of a good life but with less knowledge, a person tend to have the worse off life.

Parable or Saying:	*Mi ná Jakas!*
Translation:	*I am a Jackass!*
Interpretation:	Someone who makes a fool of himself, without realizing it, or actually thinking he/she is doing something cool.

Parable or Saying:	*Ná kɔs fɔ bi ignɔrant.*
Translation:	*It is an insult to be ignorant.*
Interpretation:	A person who is unaware of a situation and it is often used as an insult to describe an individual who deliberately ignore or disregard important information or facts.

Parable or Saying:	*Af ɛdikeshɔn denja pas wɛ yu nɔ gɛt ɛni ɛdikeshɔn.*
Translation:	*Half education is more dangerous than no education.*
Interpretation:	Small amount of knowledge can mislead people into thinking that they are more expert than they really are.

Parable or Saying:	*Stɔn wɛ de bɔtɔm watasai nɔ no sɛ ren de kam.*
Translation:	*A stone at the bottom of the river does not know it is raining.*
Interpretation:	Sheltered person does not know true hardship or trouble.

Parable or Saying: *Daiman nɔ no ɔmɔs shraud kɔs.*

Translation: *The corpse does not know the cost of her shroud.*

Interpretation: Small amount of knowledge can mislead people into thinking that they are more expert than they really are.

IGNORE, DISREGARD OR SNUB

Parable or Saying: *Ná wɛ yu luk yawo in fes, ná im yu go no sɛ ĩ de crai.*

Translation: *It is when you look at a bride's face you will know that she is crying.*

Interpretation: A person who refuses to take notice of or acknowledge someone or to disregard someone intentionally.

IMITATE, COPY OR MIMIC

Parable or Saying: *Wɛtin bifo fut de du ná im biɛn fut de fala.*

Translation: *Whatever the front feet are doing, the back feet are doing the same.*

Interpretation: A person who follows a pattern, model, or example.

Parable or Saying: *Di pɔsin wɛ de bifo pan ɛnitin ná im di wan dɛn wɛ de biɛn de fala.*

Translation: *Sometimes, everybody follows the leader.*

Interpretation: People who copy or imitate the style and behavior of the leader.

IMPERFECT, DEFECTIVE, DEFICIENT OR FAULTY

Parable or Saying: *ɔs gɛt fo fut bɔt ĩ de fɔdɔm.*

Translation: *The horse has four feet but it falls anyway.*

Interpretation: Someone or something that has at least one fault.

IMPORTANT, ESSENTIAL OR SIGNIFICANT

Parable or Saying: *Ĩ gɛt big fish fɔ frai.*

Translation: *He/she has a bigger fish to fry.*

Interpretation: He/she has more important things to do.

IMPOSSIBLE OR IMPRACTICAL

Parable or Saying: *Yu nɔ go tek natai fɔ frai stɔn.*

Translation: *You will not take nut-oil to fry stone.*

Interpretation: If an action or event is impossible, it cannot happen or be achieved.

Parable or Saying: *Nobɔdi nɔ go luk fɔ nidul ná drai bondul gras.*

Translation: *No one looks for a needle in a hay stack.*

Interpretation: Something that is extremely difficult or impossible to find.

INCOMPATIBLE, MISMATCHED OR UNSUITED

Parable or Saying: *Oyl ɛn wata nɔ de miks.*

Translation: *Oil and water do not mix.*

Interpretation: Some people or things that are incompatible by nature.

INDIVIDUAL, DISTINCT, ORIGINAL, SEPARATE OR SINGLE

Parable or Saying: *Dans to di bit.*

Translation: *Dance to the beat of the drum.*

Interpretation: Do your own thing no matter what everyone else is doing. Be an individual.

INDULGE, PAMPER OR SPOIL

Parable or Saying: *Wɛ yu gi wan man plɛnti rop, ĩ go ɛng im sɛf.*

Translation: *Give a man enough rope and he will hang himself.*

Interpretation: If one gives somebody enough freedom of action, he may destroy himself by foolish actions.

INFERIOR, MEDIOCRE, SECOND-RATE,

Parable or Saying: *Nobɔdi nɔ go mek yu fil lɛk sɛkɔn klas sitizin pas yu gi am di chans.*

Translation: *No one can make you feel inferior without your consent.*

Interpretation: A person who is lower in rank, not good or not as good as someone or something else.

Parable or Saying:	*Ná aw yu mek yusεf dèn go kɔl yu fɔ tɔn fufu ná awujoh.*
Translation:	*It is how you conduct yourself that you will be selected to prepare a pot of African cassava paste, "fufu" during an African feast known as, "Awujoh".*
Interpretation:	Developing a strong sense of self-respect can help you fulfill your potential, develop healthy relationships, and make everyone around you, see you as a person who is worthy of respect. If you respect yourself, others will respect you.

Parable or Saying:	*Nɔ tek badyai luk bεringrɔn.*
Translation:	*Do not eye roll your eyes to look at cemetery.*
Interpretation:	A deliberate way of showing lack of respect or a person who thinks that everyone is below his/her standard.

INFLUENCE, CONVINCE, CONTROL, MANIPULATE, SWAY OR WIN

Parable or Saying:	*Wan rɔtin binch pwεl di plasas.*
Translation:	*One rotten bean is enough to spoil the entire palaver sauce.*
Interpretation:	A bad person influences everyone he or she comes into contact with, making them bad too.

Parable or Saying:	*Wan rɔtin apul pwεl di rεst.*
Translation:	*One rotten apple spoils the rest.*
Interpretation:	A person's negative behavior can affect a whole group of people, influencing them to have a similar negative attitude or to engage in the same bad behavior.

Parable or Saying: *Wɛ yu fɔdɔm ná wata, yu gɛt fɔ swim.*

Translation: *When you fall into the river you must swim.*

Interpretation: A person influencing someone else, by changing the person or thing in an indirect but important way.

Parable or Saying: *Wɛ yu lidɔm wit dɔg, yu grap wit flis.*

Translation: *If you lie down with a dog you will get up with fleas.*

Interpretation: If you associate with bad company some of their crimes, misdemeanors or habits will rub off on you and you will end up like them to some degree.

Parable or Saying: *Wɛ yu rɔn wit wulf, yu go lan fɔ ala.*

Translation: *If you go with wolves, you will learn to holler or howl.*

Interpretation: The company you keep reflects your personality. A smart person surrounds himself with other smart people. If you hang out with trash, you will be perceive as trash and bad company will influence your good behavior.

Parable or Saying: *Wɛ yu go ná sɔm kɔntri wɛ dèn de dans wit wan fut, yusɛf trai fɔ dans wit wan fut.*

Translation: *When visiting a country where the people dance on one foot, you should dance on one foot.*

Interpretation: The power to change someone's behavior without directly forcing the person.

Parable or Saying: *Nɔ fɔdɔm ná wata ɛn tɔn fish.*

Translation: *Do not fall into the river and turn into a fish.*

Interpretation: Someone having the capacity to influence someone else by changing the person behavior in an indirect but important way.

Parable or Saying:	*Wε ayεn ɔt, ná im fɔ wap am.*
Translation:	*When the iron is hot you can either mold it into different shapes or cut it into separate pieces.*
Interpretation:	To take an action quickly at a good opportune time.

Parable or Saying:	*Sɔri pipul lεk kɔmpin.*
Translation:	*Misery likes company.*
Interpretation:	Unhappy people like other people to be unhappy too.

Parable or Saying:	*Nɔ fɔdɔm ná watasai εn tɔn fish.*
Translation:	*Do not fall into a river and become a fish.*
Interpretation:	A person who is influenced by others.

INJUSTICE, BONDAGE OR SLAVERY

Parable or Saying: **Mɔŋki wok, babu yit.**

Translation: *Monkey works really hard and the baboon receives the reward.*

Interpretation: A situation in which there is no fairness and justice.

Parable or Saying: **Wok fɔ Yando.**

Translation: *The deprived works very hard, but the wealthy receives the reward.*

Interpretation: A situation in which a person has absolute power over the life, fortune, and liberty of another.

Parable or Saying: **Krɔkrɔ de slev fɔ yɔs.**

Translation: *A malignant pustulent itch works hard to eradicate frambesia.*

Interpretation: A person who labors against his will for poor rations.

Parable or Saying:	*Men dɔg fɔ gɔvamɛnt.*
Translation:	*One who takes care of a dog that belongs to the government.*
Interpretation:	A person who labors against his willpower.

Parable or Saying:	*Raid wilin ɔs sotɛ yu kil am.*
Translation:	*One who rides a willing horse to death.*
Interpretation:	A person who works very hard for someone endlessly, doing something difficult and tiring, especially physical work.

Parable or Saying:	*Yu de wok lɛk Jakas.*
Translation:	*You are working like a Jackass.*
Interpretation:	A person who works very hard to survive.

Parable or Saying:	*Jakas sɛ di wɔl nɔ lɛvul.*
Translation:	*The Jackass says that the world is not a level ground.*
Interpretation:	The inequality, unfairness or injustice in distribution of opportunities and income among people in the world makes the rich get richer and the poor get poorer.

Parable or Saying:	*Trɔki sɛ di wɔl nɔ lɛvul.*
Translation:	*The turtle or tortoise says that the world is not a level ground.*
Interpretation:	The extreme poverty and those that are robbed of their basic freedom constitute an injustice of people around the world.

Parable or Saying: *Ná fɔl kotos, kakroch nɛva win di kes.*

Translation: *In the fowl's court, a cockroach never wins its case.*

Interpretation: The intense hardship and those that are robbed of their basic freedom amount to the unfairness of people around the world.

Parable or Saying: *Ná kotos, Jakas nɛva win di kes.*

Translation: *In the court of law, the Jackass never wins its case.*

Interpretation: The severe distress and those that are deprived of their basic freedom constitute inequality of people around the world.

INSENSITIVE, HARD OR THIN-SKINNED

Parable or Saying: *Man ná lɛk panwayn: wɛ ĩ yɔŋ, ĩ swit ɛn ĩ nɔ trɔŋ, wɛ ĩ ol, ĩ tron ɛn gɛtnaan.*

Translation: *Man is like palm-wine; when young, sweet but without strength, in old age, strong but harsh.*

Interpretation: Someone who is very sensitive, easily insulted and unable to deal with anything that might be seen as criticism.

INSINUATE, IMPLICATE OR IMPLY

Parable or Saying: *Int no im masta ɛn kabaslɔt no im mises.*

Translation: *Hint knows its master and a long, Creole traditional female African print dress "kabaslot", knows its mistress.*

Interpretation: An action of making something known, especially in an indirect way or an indirect indication or intimation.

INSPIRATION, ENCOURAGEMENT, MOTIVATION OR STIMULATION

Parable or Saying: *Wɛ Gɔd de fɔ yu, di dɛbul nɔ go du yu natin.*

Translation: *When God is for you, the devil can't do you any harm.*

Interpretation: If you choose to follow and love God, all things will work together for good even when things seem hopeless.

Parable or Saying: *Biɛn wan big man wɛ dòn mek am, ná wan big uman wɛ dòn ɛp am.*

Translation: *Behind a great man there is a great woman.*

Interpretation: Men's success often depends on the work and support of their wives.

INSUFFICIENT, DEFICIENT OR NOT ENOUGH

Parable or Saying: *Kaki nɔ du fɔ steshɔn masta, pɔta sɛ i waŋ loŋ trɔsis.*

Translation: *A khaki material is not enough to sew the station master's uniform and the porter is requesting a long pants uniform.*

Interpretation: Someone not having or providing enough of what is needed.

Parable or Saying: *Fud wɛ ná fɔ wan man, ná stavashɔn fɔ tu man.*

Translation: *A food for one man is starvation for two.*

Interpretation: The quantity of something is not available to fulfill a need or requirement.

INSULT, ABUSE OR RUDENESS

Parable or Saying:	*Tik ɛn stoŋ go brɔk mi bɔn bɔt wɛtin yu de tɔk nɔ go at mi.*
Translation:	*Sticks and stones may break my bones but names or words will never hurt me.*
Interpretation:	Verbal insult will not physically hurt an individual.

INTERFERE, GET IN THE WAY OR OBSTRUCT

Parable or Saying:	*Wɛ ĩ nɔ brɔk nɔ fiks am.*
Translation:	*If it is not broken do not try to fix it.*
Interpretation:	If there is no evidence of a real problem, and fixing the problem would not effectively improve the situation then do not waste time and energy trying to fix it.

Parable or Saying:	*Dèn de kɔnt yams bai dɔzin koko de rol go de.*
Translation:	*They are counting yams in dozens and cocoyams are dribbled in the counts.*
Interpretation:	Know who you are and do not step over boundary.

INVESTMENTS, ASSETS OR SAVINGS

Parable or Saying:	*Pikin ná Gɔd gif.*
Translation:	*Children are the reward of life.*
Interpretation:	Children are a blessing from the Lord. They add a special joy to the lives of everybody.

IRRELEVANT, INSIGNIFICANT OR UNIMPORTANT

Parable or Saying: *Dèn de kɔnt yams bai dɔzin koko de rol go de.*

Translation: *They are counting yams in dozens and cocoyams are dribbling in the counts.*

Interpretation: Know who you are (rank, age, status, etc.) and don't cross boundary.

IRRITATE, HURT, INFLAME OR STING

Parable or Saying: *Di fud wɛ swit gɔt mɔt, ná im go rɔn in bɛlɛ.*

Translation: *What tastes sweet in goat's mouth will later upset his or her stomach.*

Interpretation: Matters that appear all right now could hurt you later.

JUDGE OR CRITIQUE

Parable or Saying: *Nɔ jɔj buk bai in kɔba.*

Translation: *You cannot judge a book by its cover.*

Interpretation: You need to really know a person before judging.

Parable or Saying: *Wata wɛ nɔ de rɔn ná im dip.*

Translation: *Still water runs deep.*

Interpretation: A quiet person is often a deep thinker.

Parable or Saying: *Si mi ɛn kam tap wit mi, ná tu difrɛn tin.*

Translation: *To see me and come live with me are two different things.*

Interpretation: A person should be mindful of the choices he or she makes as sometimes appearance can be deceiving.

Parable or Saying: *Nɔ lisin to makit nɔis.*

Translation: *Do not listen to the noise of the market.*

Interpretation: Do not be misled by others' excitement; use the facts to judge something for yourself.

JUSTICE, FAIRNESS, HONESTY OR INTEGRITY

Parable or Saying: *Wɛtin gud fɔ di gus, ī gud fɔ di ganda.*

Translation: *What is good for the goose, is good for the gander.*

Interpretation: What is good for one type is equally good for another type, despite any irrelevant differences between the types.

KINDNESS OR GENTLENESS

Parable or Saying: *Kainɛs de mɛn sofut.*

Translation: *Kindness heals wounds.*

Interpretation: A person with a pleasant disposition, and concern for others. Act of kindness does not only benefit the receiver of the kind act, but also the giver who feels content and relax when such act is committed.

Parable or Saying: *Watasai kin flɔ oba, ná so kainɛs in sɛf tan.*

Translation: *A river sometimes overflows, so does kindness.*

Interpretation: A man's kindness sometimes is like raindrops at first and then eventually overflowing like a river.

Parable or Saying:	*Yu si tidɛ, yu nɔ si tumara bɔt lɛf am gi Gɔd.*
Translation:	*We have seen today, tomorrow is in the hands of God.*
Interpretation:	Do all the good you can, by all the means you can, in all the ways you can, in all the places you can, to all the people you can today. You must not worry yourself about tomorrow, but rather seek God's Kingdom first.

KNOWLEDGE, FACTS, INFORMATION, KNOW-HOW UNDERSTANDING

Parable or Saying:	*Buk lanin ná powa.*
Translation:	*Knowledge is power.*
Interpretation:	Knowledge is a powerful factor which helps man to attain success, power and position in life. The more one knows, the more one can control any state of affairs.

Parable or Saying:	*Buk lanin bɛtɛ pas jɛntri.*
Translation:	*Knowledge is better than riches.*
Interpretation:	A person can get rich by his knowledge but rich cannot buy knowledge. Knowledge takes care of someone, judges, increases friendship and enlightens the heart.

Parable or Saying:	*Wɛ yu nɔ no wan tin, yu go no ɔda tin.*
Translation:	*He who does not know one thing knows another.*
Interpretation:	No one knows everything but everyone knows something.

Parable or Saying:	*Buk lanin ná lɛk gadin, yu gɛt fɔ plant ná di gadin bifo yu rut di plant dèm.*
Translation:	*Knowledge is like a garden if it is not cultivated, it cannot be harvested.*
Interpretation:	If you don't make an effort to gain knowledge then don't expect to have facts, information or skills acquired through experience or education.

Parable or Saying:	Ná di pɔsin wɛ wɛr di *sus no usai de pinch am.*
Translation:	*The wearer knows where the shoe pinches.*
Interpretation:	Only the person who is suffering from anything can feel the pain.

Parable or Saying:	*Kapu sɛns nɔ kapu wɔd.*
Translation:	*Gather wisdom but do not speak a lot.*
Interpretation:	Strive for knowledge but fewer words.

Parable or Saying:	*Smol buk lanin ná bad tin.*
Translation:	*A small amount of knowledge is a dangerous thing.*
Interpretation:	A little knowledge can mislead people into thinking that they are more expert than they really are.

Parable or Saying:	*Di gɔm ná im no bɔt di tit.*
Translation:	*The gum understands the teeth affairs.*
Interpretation:	Someone who understands and aware of the nature, and significance of the situation.

Parable or Saying:	*Bifo bɔd flai á dɔn no ɔmɔs eg de ná in bɛlɛ.*
Translation:	*Even before a bird flies, one can identify the amount of eggs in her stomach.*
Interpretation:	**A person who has the idea to know what the other person is thinking.**

Parable or Saying:	*Wetin de pan yams wɛ nɛf nɔ sabi?*
Translation:	*What is inside a white-yam that a knife doesn't know about?*
Interpretation:	**Someone who investigates and understands the situation or subject. Aware or familiar with the subject.**

LAZINESS, IDLENESS, LACK OF INTEREST, LETHARGY OR SLUGGISHNESS

Parable or Saying: *Wɛ yu nɔ sabi plant, yu go dai wit angri.*

Translation: *When you do not cultivate your field, you will die of hunger.*

Interpretation: A person who is unwilling to work or unwilling to use any effort will starve to death.

Parable or Saying: *Kɔpɔ ɔ mɔni nɔ di gro pantap tik.*

Translation: *Money does not grow on trees; one earns his living by working.*

Interpretation: Someone who is unwilling to work and wants to depend on others.

Parable or Saying: *Gras nɔ di gro pantap tifman nos.*

Translation: *Grass does not grow on the nose of a thief.*

Interpretation: You should not waste money because it scarce and money cannot be obtained easily.

LEARN, BE TAUGHT, BE TRAINED, DISCOVER OR GAIN KNOWLEDGE

Parable or Saying: *Wɛ yu lan, yu go tich.*

Translation: *He who learns, teaches.*

Interpretation: As you learn, you can also teach and be a teacher.

LIE, DECEIT, DECEPTION, DISHONESTY OR FABRICATE

Parable or Saying: *Lai man kin fɔgɛt.*

Translation: *A liar needs a good memory.*

Interpretation: A dishonest person can't remember to keep his story straight.

Parable or Saying: *Lai nɔ gɛt lɛg ɔ fut, bɔt ĩ gɛt wings.*

Translation: *A lie has no leg or foot, but scandalous wings.*

Interpretation: When a person lies; obviously the lie needs another lie to support it because a lie has no leg to support it to stand; but it has wings and can fly, far and wide.

Parable or Saying: *Nɔbɔdi nɔ de biliv lai man.*

Translation: *No one believes a liar even when he or she says the truth.*

Interpretation: If people think you are a liar, they will not believe anything you say.

LIFE OR EXISTENCE

Parable or Saying:	*Kɛnɛri pre fɔ fayn fɛda, tolotolo pre fɔ lɔŋ laif.*
Translation:	*The charming canary prayed for beautiful feathers whilst the unattractive turkey prayed for long life.*
Interpretation:	Beauty is skin deep but it is life that matters.

Parable or Saying:	*Laif prɛshɔs O!*
Translation:	*Life is precious.*
Interpretation:	Life is sacred because we are made of God's image. Life is as precious as you make it. The value of life depends on what value, you give it.

Parable or Saying:	*Laif shot ɛn ful wit sɔfut.*
Translation:	*Life is short and full of blisters.*
Interpretation:	An object that blocks one's way, prevents or hinders progress in life.

Parable or Saying:	*Laif tan lɛk stɔm.*
Translation:	*Life is like a storm.*
Interpretation:	No one knows what will happen in the next moment of their lives, life changes as quickly as a storm does.

Parable or Saying:	*Laif ná ɛmti drim.*
Translation:	*Life is but an empty dream.*
Interpretation:	Life is the period between birth and death of a living thing, especially a human being.

Parable or Saying:	*Laif ná ɔp ɛn dɔŋ.*
Translation:	*Life clearly does offer its Ups and its Downs.*
Interpretation:	Life is not linear. Life's Ups and Downs makes a person strong and can conquer anything.

Parable or Saying:	*Laif kin mek yu de wit pipul wɛ kia fɔ yu.*
Translation:	*Life can surround you with people who care.*
Interpretation:	Life can surround you with good people who will inspire you to be a better person, provide you with motivation to achieve your goals, empower you to make the changes you need to succeed and cheer on your success.

LIMIT, EDGE OR MAXIMUM

Parable or Saying:	*Ná di las strɔ, ná im brɔk di kamɛl im bak.*
Translation:	*It is the final straw that breaks the camel's back.*
Interpretation:	There is a limit to everything. Doing something once too many can cause disaster. (It is like an overloaded camel whose back is broken when someone adds one straw to his or her load).

Parable or Saying:	**Plasas dòn pas rɛs.**
Translation:	*A bowl of palava/palaver sauce surpasses a plate of cooked rice.*
Interpretation:	When a person has something building up and really stressed out, the smallest thing that someone does can push him or her off the edge.

Parable or Saying:	**Wata dòn pas flawa.**
Translation:	*A cup of water surpasses a bowl of flour.*
Interpretation:	When additional demand caused a system to collapse.

LISTEN OR PAY ATTENTION

Parable or Saying:	*Set yu mɔt ɛn lisin; tɔk, tɔk nɔ fayn.*
Translation:	*One must talk little, and listen a great deal.*
Interpretation:	Someone who does not talk much, but listen to other people, probably has experience, knowledge and good judgement.

LOVE, ADORE, BE DEVOTED TO OR WORSHIP

Parable or Saying:	*Luv blain.*
Translation:	*Love is blind.*
Interpretation:	When people are in love, they do not see things realistically.

Parable or Saying:	*Luv nɔ no bɛn wes.*
Translation:	*Love does not see crooked hips.*
Interpretation:	Those in love are blind to each other's faults.

Parable or Saying:	*Wɛ yu lɛk sɔmbɔdi wɛ nɔ lɛk yu, ná lɛk yu de trowɛ wata ná dɔks bak.*
Translation:	*To love someone who does not love you is like pouring water on a duck's back.*
Interpretation:	The action is useless, waste of time or has no effect.

Parable or Saying:	*Wɛ yu fid man ĩ go lɛk yu.*
Translation:	*The way to a man's heart is through his stomach.*
Interpretation:	Feed a man well and he will love you.

Parable or Saying:	*Ĩ gɛt gud at fɔ pipul.*
Translation:	*Open heart and open mind individual.*
Interpretation:	Someone who is willing to accept new people in his or her life or someone with the spark of a kind love.

LOVERS OR DEVOTED TO

Parable or Saying:	*Ol faya wud kin kach kwik.*
Translation:	*Old firewood ignites quickly.*
Interpretation:	It's easier to rekindle a romantic relationship than to start a new one with someone new.

Parable or Saying:	*Wɛ yu fid man ĩ go lɛk yu.*
Translation:	*The way to a man's heart is through his stomach.*
Interpretation:	Feed a man well and he will love you.

LUCK, DESTINY OR FORTUNE

Parable or Saying: *ɛvri dɔg gɛt in de.*

Translation: *Every dog has his day.*

Interpretation: My turn is today, yours is tomorrow.

MAN, CHAP, GENTLEMAN, GUY OR MALE

Parable or Saying: *Man ná lɛk panwayn; wɛ ĩ yɔŋ, ĩ swit ɛn ĩ nɔ trɔŋ, wɛ ĩ ol, ĩ troŋ ɛn gɛt ná an.*

Translation: *Man is like palm-wine; when young, sweet but without strength; in old age, strong but harsh.*

Interpretation: Someone who is very sensitive, easily insulted and unable to deal with anything that might be seen as criticism.

Parable or Saying: *Biɛn wan big man wɛ dòn mek am, ná wan big uman wɛ dòn ɛp am.*

Translation: *Behind a great man there is a great woman.*

Interpretation: Men's success often depends on the work and support of their wives.

Parable or Saying: *Man wɛ nɔ gɛt wɛf, ná palampo.*

Translation: *A man without a wife, is like a vase without flowers.*

Interpretation: A man without a wife is incomplete just like a vase without flowers that is incomplete because it is not doing its work.

MARRIAGE, MATRIMONY OR WEDDING

Parable or Saying: **Mared bɛtɛ pas wɛ yu grap nia ɛmti pila.**

Translation: *Marriage is better than waking up next to an empty pillow.*

Interpretation: The legal union of a man and woman as husband and wife will make you a lot happier than living single. This is because, in a good relationship, both the good and bad experiences are shared.

Parable or Saying: **Mared ná slipul-nɔt.**

Translation: *Marriage is not a fast knot but a slip knot.*

Interpretation: Marriage is a true lovers' knot or slip knot which symbolize the connection between two couple in love.

Parable or Saying: **Mared ná sakrifaise ɛn kɔmitmɛnt.**

Translation: *Marriage is sacrifice and commitment.*

Interpretation: Genuine love involves sacrifice. When we love someone, we commit to giving ourselves totally to the other person. (**For better, for worse**).

MISTAKE, ERROR OR FAULT

Parable or Saying: *Nɔ luk usai yu fɔdɔm bɔt luk usai yu slipul.*

Translation: *Do not look where you fell but where you slipped.*

Interpretation: If you make a mistake, look at what made you to make that mistake and then try not to make the same mistake again.

Parable or Saying: *Mistek ná gud ticha.*

Translation: *Mistakes are good teachers.*

Interpretation: Mistakes are a natural part of learning. If you never make mistakes, you are not trying hard enough or taking necessary risks to become the teacher you deserve to be.

MONEY, CASH OR CURRENCY

Parable or Saying: *Wε insai yu rait an de krach, ná lɔk.*

Translation: *If the right palm of the hand itches, it signifies the coming of great luck.*

Interpretation: When the right palm of the hand itches it signifies that money you will be receiving money in the future.

Parable or Saying: *Wε yu lεk mɔni, yu gεt fɔ wok.*

Translation: *He who loves money must labor.*

Interpretation: A person should work hard to achieve.

Parable or Saying: *Mɔni ná im de tɔk.*

Translation: *Money talks.*

Interpretation: If you have a lot of money, it gives you power and influence.

Parable or Saying: *Sup swit, sup swit ná mɔni kil am.*

Translation: *Delicious soup is expensive but worth it.*

Interpretation: Spending money gives an individual power, respect and happiness.

Parable or Saying: **Mɔni gɛt wiŋg.**

Translation: *Money has wings.*

Interpretation: Do something with your money: Invest or save your money to have it multiplied before it flies away like an eagle.

Parable or Saying: **Mɔni shap pas sɔd.**

Translation: *Money is sharper than sword.*

Interpretation: Money is more powerful and it can be potentially damaging than a sword.

MOTIVATION, DRIVE OR INSPIRATION

Parable or Saying: **Di bɔd wɛ go ná di ples fɔs go gɛt ɔl di tumbu.**

Translation: *The early bird catches the most worms.*

Interpretation: If you want to achieve your goal, you must get an early start.

Parable or Saying: **Di ɔs wɛ go ná di watasai fɔs go driŋk di gud wata.**

Translation: *The horse that arrives early by the river drinks the best water.*

Interpretation: Whoever arrives first has the best chance of success.

NEED, NECESSITATE, REQUIRE OR WANT

Parable or Saying: **Waŋt, waŋt nɔ gɛt; gɛt, gɛt nɔ waŋt.**

Translation: *You want and don't have, you have and don't want.*

Interpretation: The economically disadvantage people (have-nots) are in need and those who have don't want.

Parable or Saying: *Wε yu sik, yu nɔ go tɔn dɔŋ εni dɔkta.*

Translation: *He who is sick will not refuse to see any doctor.*

Interpretation: Someone requires something because it is essential or very important.

NEVER, NO WAY, NOT AT ALL OR NOT EVER

Parable or Saying: *Wε fɔl gεt tit.*

Translation: *When chicken or fowl has teeth.*

Interpretation: Never!

NEWS, BAD NEWS OR GOSSIP

Parable or Saying: *Kongosa kin prεd kwik.*

Translation: *Bad news spread quickly.*

Interpretation: People tend to circulate bad news very quickly.

Parable or Saying: *Á nɔ gεt natin fɔ sε.*

Translation: *No news is good news.*

Interpretation: If you are waiting for news about someone, it's probably good if you hear nothing because no news is good news.

NO FAVORITISM, NO DISCRIMINATION, NO PARTIALITY OR NO PREFERENCE

Parable or Saying: *Wεtin ren mit, ná im ĩ de sok.*

Translation: *When it rains, it soaks everything it meets.*

Interpretation: Treat everyone the same.

NOSY OR TAKE NOTICE OF EVERYTHING

Parable or Saying: *Yes nɔ gɛt kɔba.*

Translation: *Ears have no cover up.*

Interpretation: Eager to listen to what someone is going to say.

OBEY, CONFORM, FOLLOW OR SUBMIT

Parable or Saying: *Á de dans tu di miuzik.*

Translation: *Dance according to the music.*

Interpretation: To always do what someone else tells you to do, whether you agree with it or not.

Parable or Saying: *Á de dans tu di tiun.*

Translation: *I am dancing to the tune.*

Interpretation: To always obey someone who has power over you.

OLD, ANCIENT, ARCHAIC, FORMER OR ONE-TIME

Parable or Saying: *Ol faya wud kin kach kwik.*

Translation: *Old firewood ignites quickly.*

Interpretation: It's easier to rekindle a romantic relationship than to start a new one with someone new.

OPPORTUNITY, CHANCE OR PROSPECT

Parable or Saying: *Wɛ yu lɔs yu chans, yu nɔ go gɛt am bak.*

Translation: *Opportunity once lost will never be regained.*

Interpretation: You will only have one chance to do something important or profitable, a chance that will never occur again.

Parable or Saying: *Tek wɛtin yu gɛt, tɛ yu gɛt wɛtin yu waŋt.*

Translation: *Take what you can get, until you can get what you want.*

Interpretation: Every opportunity well used can be a stepping stone to your ultimate goals.

Parable or Saying: *Wap di ayɛn wɛ ĩ ɔt.*

Translation: *Strike the iron while it is hot.*

Interpretation: Take advantage of the opportunity.

ORDER, COMMAND, DIRECTION OR INSTRUCTION

Parable or Saying: *Babu ɔda mɔŋki; mɔŋki ɔda ĩ tel.*

Translation: *Baboon orders monkey, monkey orders his tail.*

Interpretation: A person receives orders and deliberately passes the orders to someone else.

OWNERSHIP, POSSESSION OR RIGHTS

Parable or Saying: *Brɔko kunu ná waf, gɛt ona. No mata aw ĩ tan in masta waŋt am so.*

Translation: *A broken canoe in a wharf has its owner.*

Interpretation: The legal rights to possess something.

PARENTS, BLOOD RELATIONS, CLOSE
RELATIVES, FATHERS OR MOTHERS

Parable or Saying: *ɛlifant nɛba fel fɔ kɛr in trɔŋk.*

Translation: An *elephant never* fails to *carry its* tusk.

Interpretation: Parents never get tired of helping and supporting their children as long as they are living.

PATIENCE, ENDURANCE, PATIENT
OR TOLERANCE

Parable or Saying: *If yu tek tɛm kil anch, yu go si in gɔt.*

Translation: *If you take your time to kill an ant, you will see its intestines.*

Interpretation: Take the necessary time to investigate and you will get the answers you are seeking

Parable or Saying: *Pashɛnt dɔg yit fat bon.*

Translation: *A patient dog eats the fattest bone.*

Interpretation: One who exercises patience, that is, not insisting on immediate results, but accepting additional time to achieve a particular goal.

Parable or Saying: *Da bad man wɛ de slip nia in wɛf bɛtɛ pas ɛmti bed.*

Translation: *An awful husband sleeping besides his wife is better than an empty bed.*

Interpretation: Getting only part of what you want is better than not getting anything.

Parable or Saying: *Bo push lili bit.*

Translation: *Move a little bit is better than a wife sleeping in an empty bed.*

Interpretation: Something is better than nothing, even if it is less than one wanted.

Parable or Saying: *Bad bush nɔ de fɔ trowɛ bad pikin.*

Translation: *A child with bad behavior may not be the best child but you cannot place him/her in an unsafe place to be cared for.*

Interpretation: A child with bad behavior may not be disowned. Parents should be patient and try to shape a child's behavior.

Parable or Saying: *Put yams ná faya de luk fɔ nɛf.*

Translation: *Bring a pot of yams to a boil and patiently search for a knife.*

Interpretation: What you have now is better than something you do not have at all.

Parable or Saying: *Bɔd ná yu an bɛtɛ pas tu bɔd ná bush.*

Translation: *A bird in the hand is worth two in the bush.*

Interpretation: In short, what you have is better than what you don't have, and it's best not to gamble it away.

Parable or Saying:	*Lɔŋ rɔd kin tap sɔnsai.*
Translation:	*A very long road will certainly come to an end.*
Interpretation:	A situation, process, event or activity ends or when something or someone ends it, it reaches its final point, and goes no further.

Parable or Saying:	*Tit ɛn toŋ kin jam.*
Translation:	*Even the teeth and the tongue sometimes come into conflict but they will always unite to chew.*
Interpretation:	Life is too short to cry over petty issues. Live life the fullest by being patient, loving and understanding towards each other.

Parable or Saying:	*Kaka, pupu ɔ shit lɔŋ sotɛ, ī go kɔt.*
Translation:	*A very long excrete will dissociate at a point.*
Interpretation:	If an activity is at its end, it will terminate and will not continue.

Parable or Saying:	*Brɔko kunu ná waf bɛtɛ pas ɛmti waf.*
Translation:	*Even a broken canoe in a wharf is better than an empty wharf.*
Interpretation:	It is not what is required but it is better to have it than nothing at all.

Parable or Saying:	*Yu mate wɛ di slip ná di ɔdasai pan yu bed, bɛtɛ pas yu wan slip ná di bed.*
Translation:	*A bed mate who sleeps on the other side of the bed is better than being alone in bed.*
Interpretation:	It is not what is expected but it is better to have it than nothing at all.

Parable or Saying: *Put tik biɛn do fɔ di tɛm wɛ yu nɛba go kres.*

Translation: *Place a long stick behind your door and wait patiently for an intruder.*

Interpretation: One who is able to stay calm dealing with problems or difficult people.

Parable or Saying: *Bɛtɛ fɔ de wit di dɛbul yu no dan di engɛl wɛ yu nɔ sabi.*

Translation: *Better to stick with the devil that you know than the angel that you don't know.*

Interpretation: It is better to endure a situation that you are accustomed to than to risk a change for something that may be worse.

Parable or Saying: *Bɛtɛ fɔ de wit di dɛbul yu no dan di dɛbul wɛ yu nɔ sabi.*

Translation: *Better to stick with the devil that you know than the devil that you don't know.*

Interpretation: It is better to deal with something or someone familiar than deal with something or someone you don't know that might be worse.

Parable or Saying: *Niu brum swip klin bɔt di ol brum no usai di dɔti de ná ɔl di kɔna.*

Translation: *A new broom sweeps clean, but an old broom knows every corner.*

Interpretation: A new leader with a new perspective can easily see where the old leadership missed some things and deal with things that have been let go or over seen. However, the old leader knows his people and their habits and can easily take care of some situations with finesse because of aged wisdom.

Parable or Saying: *If yu tek tɛm kil anch, yu go si in gɔt.*

Translation: *If you take your time to dissect an ant, you will see its intestines.*

Interpretation: A person who is patient and able to accept or tolerate delays, problems, or suffering without becoming annoyed or anxious.

Parable or Saying: *Put mata-odo ɛn mata-pɛnsul biɛn yu bak do fɔ gaid yu os ɛn wet fɔ di tifman.*

Translation: *Place a mortar and pestle behind your back door to secure your house and wait for the thief.*

Interpretation: A person who has a dynamic ability to be quiet, calm without complaint and who waits patiently for something to happen.

Parable or Saying: *Wan yai man bɛtɛ pas natin kpatakpata.*

Translation: *One eyed man is better than none.*

Interpretation: Something is better than nothing, even if it is less than one wanted. "Hold on to what you've got".

Parable or Saying: *Man ɔ uman wɛ nɔ bɛtɛ, bɛtɛ pas wɛ yu wek nia ɛmti pila.*

Translation: *An untrustworthy husband or wife is better than waking up next to an empty pillow.*

Interpretation: A little of something is always better than nothing.

Parable or Saying: *Ĩ de gi yu lɔŋ rop.*

Translation: *He is giving you a long rope.*

Interpretation: Allowing someone to do what he or she wants, knowing that the person will probably fail or get into trouble.

Parable or Saying: *Tai kaw wit lɔŋ rop.*

Translation: *Tie a cow with a long rope.*

Interpretation: Given enough freedom to someone will most likely bring about his or her own downfall.

Parable or Saying: *Ná lili lili di bɔd kin tek fɔ bil in ose.*

Translation: *It is little by little that a bird builds its nest.*

Interpretation: The smallest daily accomplishments can make the biggest dreams come true.

Parable or Saying: *Wɛ yu waŋ fɔ yit ɛlifant wɛ kam yu wɛ, ná fɔ kɔt am pietpiet.*

Translation: *The best way to eat an elephant in your path is to cut it in small pieces.*

Interpretation: The best way to solve a problem is to take it bit by bit.

Parable or Saying: *Nɛt lɔŋ sotɛ, mɔnin go kam.*

Translation: *However long the night, it will be the break of dawn.*

Interpretation: When things are at their worst, be patient better times will come.

Parable or Saying: *Nɛt lɔŋ sotɛ, de go kam.*

Translation: *However long the night, it will be day break.*

Interpretation: Bad do not last forever.

Parable or Saying: *Rod lɔŋ sotɛ ĩ go bɛn.*

Translation: *Though the road is very long, it will curve to a certain point.*

Interpretation: A person who has the ability to stay calm without becoming aggravated when someone is not doing what he or she supposed to do.

Parable or Saying: ***Rod lɔŋ sotɛ ĩ go ɛn.***

Translation: *However long the road is, it will certainly come to an end.*

Interpretation: A person who is able to accept or tolerate delays, problems or suffering without becoming annoyed. 'Be patient your time will come'.

Parable or Saying: ***Yu nɔ gɛt fɔ bit babu sotɛ yu kil am bikɔs ĩ wɔwɔ.***

Translation: *You do not have to smack the baboon to death because of its ugliness.*

Interpretation: A person's ability to accept or tolerate delays, problems or suffering without becoming annoyed or anxious.

PAYMENT, BENEFIT, GAIN OR PROFIT

Parable or Saying: ***Fayn wɔd ná im de pul gud kɔla.***

Translation: *Saying encouraging positive words make a huge difference to someone.*

Interpretation: Good words are like honeycomb, sweet to the soul and healing to the bones.

PEACE, CALM OR TRANQUILITY

Parable or Saying: ***Kol at gɛt praiz bɔt ĩ kɔs mɔni.***

Translation: *Peace is costly but it is worth the expense.*

Interpretation: Peace gives you an inner tranquility. That is why it is worth the expense.

Parable or Saying: *Usai wud nɔ de, faya kin ɔt.*

Translation: *Where there is no wood; the fire goes out.*

Interpretation: Where there is no gossip a quarrel dies down or where there is no secret talk, argument ends.

PERPETUAL OR PERMANENT

Parable or Saying: *Yu padul go, yu padul kam; di kunu tinap tranga wan.*

Translation: *A paddle here, a paddle there, the canoe stays still.*

Interpretation: Something that continues forever in the same way. It never changes or ends.

Parable or Saying: *Mi ná watasai ston. Wɛ yu go sotɛ ɛn yu kam bak, yu go mit mi ná di sem ples.*

Translation: *Travel here and travel there; the riverside stone is still in its position.*

Interpretation: Object that is incapable of being moved. Firmly fixed or stationary.

Parable or Saying: *Di ston wɛ di wokman dèm nɔ braskitul, ná im ná di alagba ná di kɔna.*

Translation: *The stone that the builders rejected has become the very head stone of the corner.*

Interpretation: His family and friends did not recognize him as the leader. Later, they realized their mistakes and gave him his rightful position as the expert.

PERSISTENCE, DETERMINATION
OR PERSEVERANCE

Parable or Saying:	*Wɛ wan do kloz, ɔda do go opin.*
Translation:	*When the door of happiness closes, another door opens.*
Interpretation:	Life is full of its ups and its downs. Do not dwell so much on the past. Keep your head up so that you may receive new opportunities or the blessings ahead of you.

Parable or Saying:	*Mɔŋki trai sotɛ ĩ lan fɔ jomp frɔm wan tik to di ɔda tik.*
Translation:	*By trying, the monkey learns to jump from tree to tree.*
Interpretation:	The effort that is required to do something and keep doing it till the end, even if it is difficult.

PERSONALITY, SELF-ESTEEM, SELF-IMAGE
OR OPINION OF ONESELF

Parable or Saying:	*Pɔsin wɛ tink ĩ pas ɔlman ná bɔfun, ĩ nɔ de go nɔwɛ.*
Translation:	*An ego trip will never get you anywhere.*
Interpretation:	Someone who feels totally supreme or someone who does something to feel more important or better than other people. 'Self-gratification'.

Parable or Saying:	*Big tik de bɔtɔm watasai sotɛ ĩ nɔ go tɔn krɔkɔdail.*
Translation:	*No matter how long a log stays in water, it does not become a crocodile.*
Interpretation:	No matter how long you fake your personality, you will always be who you are.

PEST OR A PAIN IN THE NECK

Parable or Saying: *Uman ná lɛkɛ blankit; wɛ yu kɔba usɛf wit di blankit, ĩ go krach yu, wɛ yu trowɛ am, kol go kech yu.*

Translation: *A woman is like a blanket: If you cover yourself with it, it bothers you; if you throw it aside you will feel the cold.*

Interpretation: Someone who is annoying or difficult to deal with but at the same time she is indispensable.

Parable or Saying: *Gi mi push ná mi bak, nɔ min fɔ lɛ á gɛt ɔmbak.*

Translation: *Give me a push from my back does not mean to give me a hunchback.*

Interpretation: A person who renders help or support to someone and continues to remind him/her of the assistance.

PLEASANT, FINE, GOOD OR POLITE

Parable or Saying: *Wɛ yu waka pan gud rod wantɛm, yu go waka pan di sem gud rod egen.*

Translation: *When a road is good, it is used again.*

Interpretation: Having learned from your first time experience that it was good, you are prepared to experience greater success the second time around.

PLENTIFUL, AMPLE, EXTREMELY OR EXTENSIVELY

Parable or Saying: *Di fud wɛ swit gɔt mɔt, ná im go rɔn in bɛlɛ.*

Translation: *What tastes sweet in goat's mouth will later upset his or her stomach.*

Interpretation: Matters that appear all right now could hurt you later.

Parable or Saying: *ɔmɔs yu go lik pan tɛn pɛns sɔl?*

Translation: *How much can one man consume on ten-penny salt?*

Interpretation: There is a limit to everything. Doing something once too many can cause disaster.

POLITE, COURTEOUS, WELL-BRED OR WELL-MANNERED

Parable or Saying: Awdu, *nɔ* bai plaba.

Translation: *Expression or gesture of greeting someone should not cause any problem.*

Interpretation: It never costs anything to be polite.

POSITION, PLACE, RANK OR SPOT

Parable or Saying: *Yams kɔl komiti, koko sɛ ĩ waŋ rid di ajenda.*

Translation: *The white yams summons a meeting, cocoyam wants to read the agenda.*

Interpretation: Accept your position in society, organization and family, and everything will be alright.

POWER, FORCE, IMPOSE, MIGHT, PUSH, SHOVE OR VIGOR

Parable or Saying: **Push dòn kam pan shɔb.**

Translation: *Push comes to shove.*

Interpretation: When all the easy solutions to a problem have not worked, and something must be done or matters must be confronted when a crucial point is reached.

PRACTICE, ACTION, CARRY OUT OR DO

Parable or Saying: **Wɔd ná mɔt nɔto lod ná ed.**

Translation: *Not just words from your mouth but action.*

Interpretation: Practice what you preach. Someone who talks the talk but **does not walk the walk.**

PREJUDICE, BIGOTRY OR DISCRIMINATION

Parable or Saying: **Nɔ jɔj di buk bai in kɔba.**

Translation: *You must not judge the book by its cover.*

Interpretation: You should not prejudge the worth or value of someone or something.

Parable or Saying: **Jɔj man ɔ uman bai di wok wɛ ĩ de du.**

Translation: *You must judge a man by the work of his hands.*

Interpretation: Judge someone by his or her achievements.

Parable or Saying: *Nɔ jɔj di man ɔ uman bai aw ĩ luk.*

Translation: *You must judge a man or a woman based on appearance.*

Interpretation: Judge someone by his or her accomplishments.

Parable or Saying: *Jakas sɛ dis wɔl nɔ level.*

Translation: *Jackass says that this world is not level.*

Interpretation: Favor or privilege is part of life.

Parable or Saying: *Yu nɔ gɔ lɛk dɔg ɛn ɛt in tel.*

Translation: *You do not like a dog and hates its tail.*

Interpretation: Treating someone as inferior based on his/her race, sex, national origin, age or other characteristics.

PREPARE, GET READY, ORGANIZE OR SET UP

Parable or Saying: *Tai yu ɔja tayt.*

Translation: *Tie your small-wrap or scarf (Aso oke) really tight around your waist.*

Interpretation: Be prepared or be ready for any occurrence.

Parable or Saying: *Á kach di snɔf ɛn wɛr di krubɔmbɔ de wet fɔ yu.*

Translation: *I am chewing snuff and wearing a fisherman's shorts waiting for you.*

Interpretation: Be prepared or be ready for any occurrence.

PRIDE, ARROGANCE, CONCEIT, EGOTISM OR SUPERIORITY

Parable or Saying:	*Wɛ yu tink gud ov yusɛf ɛn yu kiales fɔ ɔda pipul, yu go fɔdɔm wan fayn de.*
Translation:	*Pride goes before destruction.*
Interpretation:	If you are too proud and overconfident, you will make mistakes leading to your defeat.

Parable or Saying:	*Wɛ yu tink gud ov yusɛf ɛn yu nɔ de trit pipul wit rɛspɛkt, yu go shem wɛ dèn nɔ gi yu rɛspɛkt.*
Translation:	*Pride goes, shame or disgrace follows.*
Interpretation:	A proud man thinks much more of himself expecting to be treated according to his own supposed worth, which treatment he seldom meets with, he is repeatedly ashamed, annoyed and resentful.

PRIORITY OR MAIN CONCERN

Parable or Saying:	*Wɛ yu ose de bɔn, no tɛm nɔ de fɔ go untin.*
Translation:	*When your house is burning there is no time to go hunting.*
Interpretation:	Something that is very important and must be dealt with before other things.

Parable or Saying:	Man *wɛ faya de bɔn in ose, nɔ de go untin fɔ kech arata.*
Translation:	*A man whose house is on fire does not go hunting for a rat.*
Interpretation:	Something or someone is more urgent or important than other things.

Parable or Saying: *Wɛ yu wach yu pɔt, yu fud nɔ go bɔn.*

Translation: *If you watch your pot, your food will not burn.*

Interpretation: The most important thing someone has to deal with, or must be done or dealt with before everything else.

PROBLEM, CRISIS, DILEMMA, TROUBLE OR SET BACK

Parable or Saying: *Wɛ yu trowɛ asis ná yu asis go fala.*

Translation: *What goes around, comes around.*

Interpretation: If you create the problem, you will be involved in the problem.

Parable or Saying: *Ren nɔ de fɔdɔm ná wan man ruf.*

Translation: *Rain does not fall on one man's roof.*

Interpretation: Trouble comes to everyone at one time or another.

Parable or Saying: *Krɔs di brij wɛ yu kam nia am.*

Translation: *Cross a bridge when you come to it.*

Interpretation: Face a problem when it arises.

PROBLEM TO BE SOLVED

Parable or Saying: *Ĩ tranga fɔ blɔ mi yon nos, den yu sɛ mek á blɔ bigul.*

Translation: *It is very difficult to blow my own nose, and you are telling me to blow a bugle.*

Interpretation: A person who is unable to take care of his/her problem will never solve someone's problem.

Parable or Saying:	*Wɛ yu want yit ɛlifant wɛ kam yu wɛ, ná fɔ kɔt am lili-lili.*
Translation:	*The best way to eat an elephant in your path is to cut it in small pieces.*
Interpretation:	The best way to solve a problem is to take it bit by bit.

Parable or Saying:	*Wɛ yu nɔ want lɛ wi tɔk dis kes, den yu miks de.*
Translation:	*If you are not part of the solution, you are part of the problem.*
Interpretation:	If you do not take direct action to make things better you are an obstacle to change.

PROOF, EVIDENCE OR VERIFICATION

Parable or Saying:	*Wɛ yu waŋ fɔ no aw di pap swit, ná fɔ tes am fɔs.*
Translation:	*The proof of the pudding is in the eating.*
Interpretation:	The real value of something can be judged only after it has been tried or tested.

PROVERBS, IDIOMS, PARABLE
OR WISE SAYINGS

Parable or Saying:	*Prɔvab ɔ parɛbul ná lɛkɛ pamayn wɛ pipul dèn lɛk fɔ yit.*
Translation:	*Proverb or parable is like palm oil with which words are eaten.*
Interpretation:	Proverb or Parable is important and essential as the food the Africans need to live on.

Parable or Saying:	*Prɔvab ɔ parɛbul ná lɛkɛ ɔs wɛ go kɛr yu ples fɔ lɛ yu no sɔmtin.*
Translation:	*Proverb or parable is like the horse that can carry one swiftly to the discovery of ideas.*
Interpretation:	Proverb or parable is important to Africans because it helps them to communicate, imagine, and understand their culture and the world in which they live.

Parable or Saying:	*Prɔvab ɔ parɛbul ná lɛkɛ gyal pikin wɛ ɔndastan parɛbul ɛn uz di parɛbul dɛm ɛveride fɔ mek in laif bɛtɛ.*
Translation:	*Proverbs are the daughters of daily experience.*
Interpretation:	Proverbs do not have to be explained to Africans. Most Africans use proverbs in their everyday conversations and they actually understand the messages that proverbs convey to sustain their lives. Such as: General truth of advice, warning, comment on human daily experience and so on.

Parable or Saying:	*Man wɛ no parɛbul go sɛtul plaba.*
Translation:	*A man who knows proverbs will reconcile differences.*
Interpretation:	An individual who handles a matter wisely, attains to the truth and happiness is someone who knows proverbs.

PROVOKE, AGGRAVATE, GET ON YOUR NERVES, INCITE OR IRRITATE

Parable or Saying:	*Wi gɛt bon fɔ pik.*
Translation:	*We have a bone to pick.*
Interpretation:	An individual who wants to talk to someone about something that he or she has done and does not know about.

PUBLICIZE, ANNOUNCE, BROADCAST
OR MAKE KNOWN

Parable or Saying: *Nɔ was yu fambul dɔti linin ná trit.*

Translation: *Home affairs are not talked about on the public square.*

Interpretation: Family should remain confidential amongst family unless it is life threatening.

Parable or Saying: *Wɛ yu nɔ opin yu winda, udat go si yu?*

Translation: *If you do not open your window, who will see you?*

Interpretation: Unless the home affairs are talked about, the public will not be aware of the situation.

Parable or Saying: *Wɛ yu nɔ opin yu do, udat go kam insai?*

Translation: *If you do not open your door, who will come in?*

Interpretation: Unless the home activities are discussed, the public will not be aware of the circumstances.

Parable or Saying: *Lɛ di pɔblik no yu apines dan yu wahala.*

Translation: *Publish your joys instead of your troubles.*

Interpretation: When somone talks about joys instead of focusing on the negative aspects of life, he or she will be able to act positively from this position and live a joyful life.

Parable or Saying: *Ĩ nɔ di put im mɔt ná bɔtul fɔ tɔk.*

Translation: *In fact, he does not position his mouth in the spout of a bottle to talk; he says everything he knows.*

Interpretation: Someone who makes everything widely known.

Parable or Saying: *Ĩ nɔ di put im mɔt ná ol fɔ tɔk.*

Translation: *In fact, he does not place his mouth in a hole to talk; he says the whole thing.*

Interpretation: The individual makes information about something generally available.

PURPOSELESS, EMPTY OR MEANINGLESS

Parable or Saying: *Om wɛ nɔ gɛt uman ná lɛk ɛmti ship ose wɛ ship nɔ tap.*

Translation: *Home without a woman is like a barn with no cattle.*

Interpretation: A home without a woman is depressing, cheerless or joyless and no one is there to be of assistance.

PUSH, FORCE, IMPOSE, MIGHT, POWER, SHOVE, STRENGTH OR VIGOR

Parable or Saying: *Push dòn kam pan shɔb.*

Translation: *Push comes to shove.*

Interpretation: When all the easy solutions to a problem have not worked, and something must be done or matters must be confronted when a crucial point is reached.

QUARREL, ARGUE, CLASH OR SQUABBLE

Parable or Saying: *Wan an banguls nɔ de shek.*

Translation: *A single bracelet does not shake.*

Interpretation: It takes two to argue or quarrel.

Parable or Saying:	*Ná Sarah plaba.*
Translation:	*She is known as Sarah the hot-tempered.*
Interpretation:	Someone who is always arguing or disagreeing with people on good terms or someone who is causing unnecessary argument.

Parable or Saying:	*Plaba go dòn bɔt wɛtin yu pul ná yu mɔt nɔ go dai.*
Translation:	*Quarrel ends but words spoken never die.*
Interpretation:	People sometimes reconcile their differences but negative words once spoken will never be recalled or replaced.

Parable or Saying:	*Gɔt kaka ɔ pupu waŋ fɔ rol, bɔt ĩ de wait fɔ sɔmbɔdi fɔ push am.*
Translation:	*A goat excrete wishes to roll down a hill, but waits for someone to give it a push.*
Interpretation:	An individual desires to have a clash or fight with someone, he or she waits for the opportune time.

Parable or Saying:	*Tit ɛn tɔŋ kin jam.*
Translation:	*Even the tongue and the teeth quarrel sometime!*
Interpretation:	It takes two or more people to quarrel. Family, friends and others could quarrel because that's the facts of life, but quarreling should not harm their relationships.

Parable or Saying:	*Tit ɛn tɔŋ kin set kitikata.*
Translation:	*If you tell two people to live together, you are telling them to quarrel.*
Interpretation:	It takes two to make a quarrel. An argument/quarrel is not only one person's fault; if the other person refuses to participate, an argument/quarrel won't occur.

Parable or Saying:	*Di faya ɔt!*
Translation:	*The fire is really hot!*
Interpretation:	Having a heated argument or disagreement.

Parable or Saying:	*Wud wɛ dòn tɔch ná faya nɔ at fɔ kech.*
Translation:	*Wood already touched by fire is not hard to set alight.*
Interpretation:	A person who already angry is easy to coax in quarreling or fighting.

QUIET, CALM, SETTLE DOWN OR SILENCE

Parable or Saying:	*Bɛt yu tɔŋ!*
Translation:	*Bite your tongue!*
Interpretation:	When a person wants to say something that may be offensive or hurtful to someone, he/she attempts not to say anything or when a person makes a conscious effort not to say anything, usually for the sake of politeness or peace.

Parable or Saying:	*Ol yu tɔŋ.*
Translation:	*Hold your tongue.*
Interpretation:	Be silent.

Parable or Saying:	*Mɔt wɛ di yit nɔ de tɔk.*
Translation:	*A mouth which eats does not talk.*
Interpretation:	When someone is busy doing something constructive rather than talking all the time will have more success.

RAISE, BRING UP, NURTURE OR REAR

Parable or Saying: *Nɔ to wan pɔsin de mɛn pikin.*

Translation: *It takes a village to raise a child.*

Interpretation: In an African village, a child is seen as a blessing from God and communal effort is employed in nurturing that child. The whole village community which includes; the child's parents, family, extended family members, friends and neighbors contribute in the upbringing of that child. For example; at different times when the parents of the child are away extended family members, friends and neighbors offer free advisory role.

REASON, CAUSE, MOTIVE OR PURPOSE

Parable or Saying: *Wɛ yu si ɔkpɔlɔ klem fench, mɔs nɔ sɛ ná wam sansan wam!*

Translation: *If a frog climbs up a fence, it is because the sand is hot.*

Interpretation: Unusual cause is responsible for a usual behavior.

Parable or Saying: *Wɛ yu si ɔkpɔlɔ klɛm tik, mɔs nɔ sɛ di grɔn ot!*

Translation: *When you see a frog climbing a tree, you must know the ground is hot.*

Interpretation: A person's condition that caused sudden unusual or strange changes in his/her behavior.

Parable or Saying: *Wɛ yu si ɔkpɔlɔ de rɔn santɛm, big snek de biɛn am.*

Translation: *When you see a frog hopping during the day, it is being chased by a snake.*

Interpretation: A person's situation that caused him to perform actions that are not normal.

RECKLESS, CARELESS, INATTENTIVE OR IRRESPONSIBLE

Parable or Saying: *If yu nɔ so yu chɛrchɛr klos, yu nɔ go gɛt ɛni klos lɛf.*

Translation: *He who does not mend his clothes will soon have none.*

Interpretation: If you sort your problem immediately, it will save you a lot of problem later.

RECONCILE, BRING TOGETHER, PATCH UP, RESOLVE OR SETTLE

Parable or Saying: *Lɛ wi bɛr di kɔtlas.*

Translation: *Let's bury the hatchet.*

Interpretation: To agree that you will forget about arguments and disagreements with someone.

Parable or Saying: *Lɛ dɔg wɛ de slip lidɔm.*

Translation: *Let's sleeping dog lie.*

Interpretation: Don't do anything that will stir up unnecessary trouble.

Parable or Saying: *Tit ɛn tɔŋ kin set kitikata bɔt dèn kin mek am ɔp.*

Translation: *Teeth and tongue do collide but later solve their problems.*

Interpretation: To settle one's differences or make it up.

Parable or Saying:	*Bifo ĩ bɔn, lɛ ĩ sok.*
Translation:	*Instead of burning the item, soak it through.*
Interpretation:	To settle or resolve. To find a way in which two situations or beliefs that are opposed to each other can agree.

REGENERATE, REAWAKEN, REKINDLE, RELIGHT, RENEW OR REVIVE

Parable or Saying:	*Ol frɛn nɔ at fɔ kam togɛda egen.*
Translation:	*Old friendship is not hard to rekindle.*
Interpretation:	Getting back together with someone that you were once together with in the past. To re-ignite a relationship with someone on more than a friendship level.

Parable or Saying:	*Ol faya wud izi fɔ kech.*
Translation:	*Old firewood is easy to relight.*
Interpretation:	To revive, renew, to arouse again with hopes or feelings which have been lost or diminished and with the anticipation to start building a good relationship.

REMEMBER OR KEEP IN MIND

Parable or Saying:	*ɛlifant nɔ de fɔgɛt.*
Translation:	*An elephant does not forget.*
Interpretation:	A person who is able to remember a fact, something that happened or how to do something.

RESPECT, ADMIRATION, HIGH OPINION
OR REVERENCE

Parable or Saying: *Pɔ man ĩ at nɔ di las lɔŋ bikɔs ĩ de tek am ɔltɛm ná ĩ ed fɔ sho rɛspɛkt.*

Translation: *A poor man's hat does not last long because he takes it off too often to pay his respects.*

Interpretation: A person who acts in a way that shows he or she cares about others feelings and well-being.

Parable or Saying: *ɔkrɔ nɔ go langa pas im masta.*

Translation: *An okra plant cannot grow taller than its master, the sower.*

Interpretation: Nobody is above his/her parent(s). "No matter how tall an okra plant is, the sower bends it to harvest its buds".

Parable or Saying: *Tu masta nɔ go drɛb wan ship.*

Translation: *Two masters will not steer a ship.*

Interpretation: To accept the importance of someone's rights and not to do anything that will harm or cause offense.

Parable or Saying: *Polisman vɛks sotɛ, ĩ nɔ go nak im bɔs.*

Translation: *No matter how angry a policeman, he will never smack his superior.*

Interpretation: A feeling or understanding that someone or something is important, valuable, worthy or significant and should be treated in an appropriate way.

Parable or Saying: *Alagba dɛn kin gladi fɔ sidɔm wit pikin wɛ gɛt trenin.*

Translation: *Elders are always happy to interact with a well raised child.*

Interpretation: A child who behaves in a way that shows regard for someone or something. A child who treat others like he or she wants to be treated.

Parable or Saying: *Ná bai di klos wɛ yu wɛr, ná im egugu go tek yu flo.*

Translation: *It is according to what you are wearing that the masked devil will run after you and eventually hit you.*

Interpretation: If you wish to earn the respect of others, your best bet is to broadcast respect for yourself and dress with care.

Parable or Saying: *Pikin wɛ sabi was in an go yit wit di alagba dèm.*

Translation: *If a child knows how to wash his or her hands, he/she would eat with kings.*

Interpretation: A young person who is disciplined and well-mannered will participate with elders.

Parable or Saying: *Wɛ yu ple wit sɔm pɔsin tomɔs, yu go lɔs yu rɛspɛkt.*

Translation: *Familiarity breeds contempt but distance breeds respect.*

Interpretation: We have the most respect for people when we do not know them intimately, or when our interactions have some degree of distance familiarity.

Parable or Saying:	*If yu nɔ lidɔm ná grɔn, nobɔdi nɔ go mas yu pas.*
Translation:	*If you don't lie down on the floor, no one can walk on you.*
Interpretation:	You have to carry yourself with respect and respect others so that they will respect you.

Parable or Saying:	*Fufu ɔ foo-foo nɔ go fityai ɔkrɔ sup.*
Translation:	*The African prepared cassava paste "fufu" will not challenge or disrespect okra soup during mealtime.*
Interpretation:	A prepared African cassava paste "fufu" strives hard not to repress a bowl of delicious, tasty, palatable okra soup but to accompany it during mealtime.

Parable or Saying:	*ɔkpɔlɔ wɛ dòn bɛful nɔ go trai fɔ chalenj yuba.*
Translation:	*A frog with a full stomach will never disrespect a vulture.*
Interpretation:	Someone who strives not to challenge his authority but work together to accomplish a specific goal.

RESPONSIBILITY, ACCOUNTABILITY, DUTY, JOB, OBLIGATION OR TASK

Parable or Saying:	*Nɔ to wan pɔsin de mɛn pikin.*
Translation:	*It takes a village to raise a child.*
Interpretation:	The whole village community, extended family members and friends contribute in the upbringing of a child.

Parable or Saying: *Gɔd nɔ go gi yu lod wɛ yu nɔ go ɛbul fɔ tot.*

Translation: *God won't give you more than you can bear.*

Interpretation: God only gives you what you can handle. He is faithful; he won't let you be tempted beyond what you can bear.

REVEAL, EXPOSE OR MAKE KNOWN

Parable or Saying: *Wɛ yu bɔn ose, yu kin ayd di smok?*

Translation: *If you burn a house, can you conceal the smoke?*

Interpretation: If you do not want anyone to know something do not tell anyone. If you tell someone that person is likely to tell others.

Parable or Saying: *Wɛ yu de ayd nɔ lait faya.*

Translation: *If you are hiding, don't light fire.*

Interpretation: If you do not want anyone to see you, do not draw attention to yourself if you do not want to be caught. Lighting a fire will get people's attention.

RICH, PROSPEROUS, WEALTHY OR WELL-OFF

Parable or Saying: *Wɛ yu waŋ fɔ jɛntri yu gɛt fɔ wok.*

Translation: *To be rich is determination and hard work.*

Interpretation: Just work hard now and you'll be richly rewarded later.

SEEING IS BELIEVING, CATCH SIGHT OF, PERCEIVE OR SET EYES ON

Parable or Saying: *Yu nɔ go bai ɔg ná pɛn.*

Translation: *You will not buy a pig in the pig's pen.*

Interpretation: Examine carefully whatever you purchase or accept from someone else.

Parable or Saying: *Yu nɔ go bai bot wɛ de ɔnda wata.*

Translation: *You do not buy a boat that is under water.*

Interpretation: Carefully examine the facts about what you are buying.

Parable or Saying: *Yu nɔ go bai kaw wɛ yu jɛs de yɛri in vɔis.*

Translation: *You do not buy a cow only by the sound of its voice.*

Interpretation: Do not be quick to accept a person as the "genuine article" without a thorough investigation.

SECRETE, HUSH-HUSH OR UNDISCLOSED

Parable or Saying: *Nɔ was yu dɔti linin ná pɔblik.*

Translation: *Do not wash your dirty linen in public.*

Interpretation: We should not discuss intimate family matters in public, especially if they are of the shameful nature.

Parable or Saying: *Lɛ dɔg drim lɛf ná im bɛlɛ.*

Translation: *A dog's dream will never be revealed.*

Interpretation: Keep secrets; secret.

SELF-CONSCIOUS, AWKWARD, INSECURE OR UNSURE OF ONESELF

Parable or Saying: *Bikɔs kɔt nos man de ná tɔŋ, yu nɔ fɔ mek hoŋ?*

Translation: *Because a man with a bit up nose is in town, you should not sneeze?*

Interpretation: A person who is excessively aware of being observed or criticized by others.

SENSE, BRAINS, INTELLECT, INTELLIGENCE OR LOGIC

Parable or Saying: *Kapu sɛns nɔ kapu wɔd.*

Translation: *Acquire wisdom instead of words.*

Interpretation: Good judgment is better than words.

SENSITIVE, AWARE, OVERSENSITIVE, RECEPTIVE OR RESPONSIVE

Parable or Saying: *Bikɔs kɔt nos man de ná tɔŋ, yu nɔ fɔ mek hoŋ?*

Translation: *Because a man with a bit up nose is in town, you should not sneeze?*

Interpretation: An oversensitive person who takes things too personally or feels defensive.

SEPARATE OR DISCONNECT

Parable or Saying: *Wɛ yu ná kɔp handul, yu gɛt fɔ tek tɛm wit di kɔp.*

Translation: *If you are the cup handle, beware of the cup.*

Interpretation: Work with your spouse as a team and set your family values. Set your boundaries and limits with your in-laws. Be at your best behavior around your in-laws.

Parable or Saying: *Wɛ yu nɔ waŋ di mɔŋki in tel fɔ tɔch yu, nɔ atend di mɔŋki dans.*

Translation: *If you do not want the monkey's tail to touch you, do not attend the monkey's dance.*

Interpretation: A person could avoid unwanted outcomes by simply not carrying out some actions.

SERIOUS OR NOT FUNNY

Parable or Saying: *Tit nɔ de munin.*

Translation: *Teeth do not mourn.*

Interpretation: A situation that requires careful thought. Important matters.

Parable or Saying: *Ple ple kil bɔd, dai bɔd kuk sup.*

Translation: *Playing continuously with someone, sometimes create problems.*

Interpretation: One person's fun and games may have serious consequences to another person.

SHAMEFUL, APPALLING OR DISGRACEFUL

Parable or Saying: ***Fɔs ful nɔto ful, bɔt sekɔn ful, ná in ná ful.***

Translation: *If you're fooled once you're not a fool, but if it happens twice, then you're a fool.*

Interpretation: **If you let a person who obviously fooled you fool you again, it is shameful.**

SHOW OFF, BIGHEAD, BOASTER OR BRAGGER

Parable or Saying: ***ɛng ɔg ed ná fench.***

Translation: *Displaying a pig's head on a fence.*

Interpretation: **A person who is trying to make an impression.**

SILLY, FOOL OR STUPID

Parable or Saying: ***Wɛ yu mek yusɛf lɛk mata ná dɔmɔt, dèn go wep dèn fut pan yu.***

Translation: *If you make yourself into a doormat, people will wipe their feet on you.*

Interpretation: **You teach people how to treat you by the way you treat yourself. If you have self-respect, people will respect you.**

SIMILAR, ALIKE, SAME KIND,
SIMILARITY OR RESEMBLANCE

Parable or Saying: *Mɔŋki dèm ná bai pati, pigin dèm ná bai pia.*

Translation: *Monkeys are by party, pigeons by pair.*

Interpretation: People who are a lot alike tend to gather together and become friends.

Parable or Saying: *Pɔŋkiŋ nɔba bia watamɛlon.*

Translation: *Pumpkin vines never produce watermelon.*

Interpretation: Children having the same or some of the same characteristics of parents.

Parable or Saying: *Orinche tik nɔ de bia lɛm.*

Translation: *An orange tree does not produce lime or lemon fruits.*

Interpretation: Children having a resemblance in appearance or nature of parents.

Parable or Saying: *Ná dɔg de bɔn dɔg.*

Translation: *A dog gives birth to a dog.*

Interpretation: When two people look like each other or are similar in some other way.

Parable or Saying: *Wata nɔ de jomp ol.*

Translation: *Water does not skip a hole.*

Interpretation: Two individuals are very like each other in some way.

Parable or Saying: *Jɔn pamayn trowɛ ná Jɔn rɛs*

Translation: *John's palm oil spilled over John's rice.*

Interpretation: When two folks' qualities or actions are the same; others try not to be involved.

Parable or Saying:	*Kaka nɔ go drɛb kaka ná grasfil, bikɔs ov ĩ bad smɛl; dèm ɔl de smɛl di sɛm.*
Translation:	*Excrete should not restrict another excrete from residing in a field because of its unpleasant smell. In fact, all of them smells the same.*
Interpretation:	When peoples' behaviors, characters, traits or actions are the same; one cannot be selective.

SINGLE, ALONE, FRIENDLESS, LONELY OR SOLITARY

Parable or Saying:	*Mi ná palampo.*
Translation:	*I am a lamp post.*
Interpretation:	A person who prefers to be alone, especially one who avoids the company of friends, girlfriends or others.

SKILLS, ABILITIES OR TALENTS

Parable or Saying:	*Nɔ ayd yu lait ɔnda bundul.*
Translation:	*Don't hide your light under a bushel.*
Interpretation:	If you have special skills or talents, do not conceal them through modesty and prevent others from appreciating or benefiting from them.

Parable or Saying:	*ɔl finga nɔ to wan.*
Translation:	*All fingers are not the same size.*
Interpretation:	People with different skills and abilities.

SLOWLY, LITTLE BY LITTLE OR STEP BY STEP

Parable or Saying: *Lan fɔ crip bifo yu waka.*

Translation: *Learn to crawl before you walk.*

Interpretation: Do the basics before trying to do things that are more complexed.

SMART, CLEVER, INTELLIGENT, NEAT, STYLISH, TIDY OR WELL-DRESSED

Parable or Saying: *Baba nɔ de shev imsɛf.*

Translation: *A barber does not shave himself.*

Interpretation: A person who makes smart and intelligent decisions.

Parable or Saying: *Wɛ yu klɛm ɔp tik, yu gɛt fɔ kam dòn di sɛm tik.*

Translation: *If you climb up a tree, you must climb down the tree.*

Interpretation: A person who is showing quick-witted intelligence.

Parable or Saying: *Wata go fɛn usai fɔ kɔmɔt.*

Translation: *Water always finds a way out.*

Interpretation: One who shows the ability to easily learn or understand things or deals with new or difficult situations.

SOLVE, GET TO THE BOTTOM OF THE PROBLEM OR RESOLVE

Parable or Saying: *Ná yu gɛt di bol ɛn di kalbas, miks wɛtin de insai.*

Translation: *The bowl and the calabash are yours; mix the contents into a desired consistency.*

Interpretation: A person who shows the ability to work through details of a problem to reach a solution.

STRIVE, DO YOUR BEST, GO ALL-OUT, MAKE EVERY EFFORT OR TRY HARD

Parable or Saying: *Yu nɔ gɛt fɔ bi di shɛp nɛf ná di bɔnch, bɔt trai.*

Translation: *You do not have to be the sharpest knife in the bunch; but do your best.*

Interpretation: Strive to accomplish your dreams. Be the best that you can be.

STUBBORN OR HEAD STRONG

Parable or Saying: *Wɛtin du, tik brɔk insai yu yes?*

Translation: *What's wrong, is there a broken stick inside your ears?*

Interpretation: Are you hard of hearing or head strong?

Parable or Saying: *Pikin wɛ sɛ ĩ mami nɔ go slip insɛf nɔ go slip.*

Translation: *A child who says his/her mother won't sleep will also be awake.*

Interpretation: You will not be at rest if you are stressing someone.

Parable or Saying: *Fɔl wɛ nɔ yɛri, "Sheee!" Ĩ go yɛri ston.*

Translation: *A rooster or hen that is not afraid of the sound "**Sheee!**" to leave a specific area will feel the stones thrown at him/her.*

Interpretation: A person with strong fear of change. Anything new, different involving change is perceived as a direct threat, even if the change in question is positive and is in the person's best interests.

Parable or Saying: *Ol sofut at fɔ mɛn.*

Translation: *Old sore is hard to cure.*

Interpretation: An individual who is unwilling to change his opinion or attitude, in spite of good reasons to.

Parable or Saying: *Nɔ trowɛ wata ná dɔks bak.*

Translation: *Do not throw water over a duck's back.*

Interpretation: A person who determines to have his own way.

Parable or Saying: *Ĩ nɔ de yɛri kɔt nos man in wɔd.*

Translation: *He/she refuses to listen to someone with a bit-up nose.*

Interpretation: A strongheaded who does not follow intstructions. A person who thinks he/she is always right.

Parable or Saying: *Da pikin wɛ sɛ ĩ go mɔna ĩ mami, ná insɛf ĩ go mɔna.*

Translation: *A child who tries to make it difficult for his mother to nurture him will be making it difficult for himself.*

Interpretation: A power struggle child who determines to do what he wants to do; learns for himself the hard way, rather than accepting his mother's instructions.

Parable or Saying: *Da pikin wɛ nɔ waŋ yɛri wud, dɛn go tich am ná trit.*

Translation: *A child who does not want to listen to his parents' instructions will be taught lessons in the street.*

Interpretation: A strong-willed child who desperately wants to be in charge of himself and does not want to co-operate with his parents will have it tough in the street.

Parable or Saying: *Yu kin tek ɔs ná watasai, bɔt yu nɔ go fos am fɔ drink wata wɛ ĩ nɔ tɔsti.*

Translation: *You can lead a horse to water, but you can't force him to drink.*

Interpretation: You can give someone an advantage or provide them with an opportunity, but you can't force them to do something if they don't want to.

Parable or Saying: *Ĩ ná abɔbɔ ĩ nɔ lɛk kolwata.*

Translation: *He is like a boiled black eyed peas that resent cold water.*

Interpretation: A strong-headed person who does not listen to authority but thinks he is always right.

Parable or Saying: *Yu nɔ go bit babu sotɛ yu kil am bikɔs ĩ wɔwɔ.*

Translation: *You cannot whack a baboon until he/she is dead because he/she is ugly.*

Interpretation: A difficult person who is resisting authority will not change his attitude, opinion or idea despite pressure to do so.

SUCCESS, ACHIEVEMENT, ACCOMPLISHMENT, WINNER, STAR OR TRIUMPH

Parable or Saying: *Wɛ yu fɔdɔm, grap, wep yu kloz ɛn trai egen.*

Translation: *When you fall, dust yourself up and try again.*

Interpretation: When you fall; get up, dust yourself and try again. Take the opportunity to venture in a different direction.

Parable or Saying: *Wɛ yu fɔdɔm, grap, wep yu klos, trai egen ɛn nɔ mek ɔda pipul tek yu lɔk.*

Translation: *When you fall, pick yourself up and try again.*

Interpretation: If at all you don't succeed; take a deep breath. Dust yourself off and try to start all over again. It will be the chance of a new beginning.

Parable or Saying: *Wan an nɔ de was insɛf.*

Translation: *One hand cannot wash itself.*

Interpretation: You need others to succeed in life.

SUPERIOR, GREATER, HIGH-CLASS OR TOP QUALITY

Parable or Saying: *Kɔntintri fɔdɔm sotɛ, ĩ pas gras.*

Translation: *Even a fallen cotton tree is taller than a weed or grass.*

Interpretation: A high-class person who is less rich nowadays is better-off than the weak or underpriviledged.

Parable or Saying:	*ɛngɛl nɔ de fityai Gɔd.*
Translation:	*An angel will not disrespect God because God is our creator and HE is more powerful.*
Interpretation:	If an individual disrespects his superior he will certainly be faces with disciplinary action.

SUPPORT, ASSISTANCE, BACKING OR ENCOURAGEMENT

Parable or Saying:	*Nɔto wan pɔsin de mɛn pikin.*
Translation:	*It takes a village to raise a child.*
Interpretation:	The whole village community, extended family members and friends contribute in the upbringing of a child.

Parable or Saying:	*Ɔl finga nɔto di sem.*
Translation:	*All fingers are not the same.*
Interpretation:	Everyone is unique and has special talent for doing the best job.

SURVIVAL, ENDURE, STAY ALIVE, SURVIVE OR UPS AND DOWNS

Parable or Saying:	*Ɔlman de padul ī yɔn kunu.*
Translation:	*Everyone paddles his own canoe.*
Interpretation:	A person who is independent and does not need help from anyone.

Parable or Saying:	*Dis ná dɔg yit dɔg wɔl.*
Translation:	*It is the dog eat dog's world.*
Interpretation:	Survival for the fittest.

Parable or Saying:	*Ná mɔŋki wɔl wi de, ol mɔŋki de jomp fɔ insɛf.*
Translation:	*In the monkey's world, each monkey jumps for himself/ herself.*
Interpretation:	You have to look out for your own interests.

Parable or Saying:	*ɛvri man fɔ insɛf ɛn Gɔd fɔ ɔl.*
Translation:	*Every man for himself and God for all.*
Interpretation:	Every man has the right for his survival. Each person should do what best for himself/herself.

SWITCH, ALTER, SUBSTITUTE, SWAP OR SWOP

Parable or Saying:	*Wɛ di miusik chenj; di dans kin chenj.*
Translation:	*The music changes; so does the dance.*
Interpretation:	When a situation changes a person will react in a certain way.

TALK, CHAT, CONVERSE, GOSSIP OR SPEAK

Parable or Saying:	*Tɔk, tɔk bɔd nɔ de bil ose.*
Translation:	*A chattering bird builds no nest.*
Interpretation:	One who talks a lot will not be able to do the best job.

Parable or Saying: **Big mɔt ɔ awoko.**

Translation: *A loud mouthed person.*

Interpretation: A talkative who speaks loudly and openly.

Parable or Saying: **Mɔt mɔt!**

Translation: *A big mouthed person.*

Interpretation: Talking too much, especially about things that should be secrete.

Parable or Saying: **Les tɔk mɔ akshɔn.**

Translation: *Less talk more action.*

Interpretation: Action speaks louder than voice.

Parable or Saying: **ɛmti vɛsul mek bɔku nɔis.**

Translation: *Empty vessels make the most noise.*

Interpretation: The least intelligent or foolish people are often the most talkatives.

Parable or Saying: **Dadi ɔ mami tɔk, tɔk!**

Translation: *He/she talks a lot.*

Interpretation: Talking too much gets one in trouble.

Parable or Saying: **Ĩ nɔ de put im mɔt ná bɔtul fɔ tɔk**

Translation: *In fact, he does not place his mouth on the spout of a bottle to voice out his opinion.*

Interpretation: A person who speaks frankly in order to give information; expresses ideas or feelings.

Parable or Saying: *Ĩ nɔ de put im mɔt ná ol fɔ tɔk wɛtin de ná im mayn.*

Translation: *In a matter of fact, he does not place his mouth in a whole; he speaks his mind.*

Interpretation: A person who speaks freely for what he believes.

Parable or Saying: *Bɔd wɛ de tɔk nɔ de yit rɛs.*

Translation: *A bird that talks does not eat rice.*

Interpretation: Someone who talks carelessly, "blabber mouth" often telling secrets to other people.

Parable or Saying: *Set yu mɔt ɛn lisin; tɔk, tɔk nɔ fayn.*

Translation: *One must talk little, and listen a great deal.*

Interpretation: Someone who does not talk much, but listen to other people has experience, knowledge and good judgement.

Parable or Saying: *Wɛ yu nɔ lɛk tɔk-tɔk uman, lɛf pan palampo*

Translation: *He who doesn't like chattering women must stay a bachelor.*

Interpretation: A person who prefers to be a bachelor because he resent women who talk rapidly in thoughtless or purposeless way.

Parable or Saying: *Tɔk, tɔk bɔd nɔ de bil ose.*

Translation: *A chattering bird builds no nest.*

Interpretation: A blabber mouth will not get the job done.

TEMPORARY, IMPERMANENT OR TRANSITORY

Parable or Saying: *Lif de rɔtin.*

Translation: *Every leaf will finally rots or withers away.*

Interpretation: Nothing is permanent in this world, not even your troubles.

THIEF, BURGLAR, PICKPOCKET, ROBBER OR SHOPLIFTER

Parable or Saying: *Ná akata de kach akata.*

Translation: *It takes a thief to catch a thief.*

Interpretation: The best person to catch a thief is another thief, because he or she knows how a thief thinks or acts.

Parable or Saying: *Tif, tif Gɔd laf.*

Interpretation: *A thief steals from another thief, God laughs.*

Interpretation: This is a situation where justice is served.

THINK, MEDITATE, REASON OR REFLECT

Parable or Saying: *Bifo bɔd flai á dòn no ɔmɔs eg de ná in bɛlɛ.*

Interpretation: *Before a bird flies off, I have already known the amount of eggs in her stomach.*

Interpretation: By the time you are thinking. I have already read your mind and arrived at the answers.

THRIFTY OR CHEAP

Parable or Saying: *Ĩ krabit lɛk spun bak.*

Interpretation: *He is as thrifty as the backside of a spoon.*

Interpretation: A person who uses money and other resources carefully and not wastefully.

TIME, INSTANCE, MOMENT, OCCASION OR PERIOD

Parable or Saying: *Tidɛ ná fɔ yu, tumara ná fɔ mi.*

Translation: *Today is for me, tomorrow is for you.*

Interpretation: What happened to you today, might happen to me tomorrow.
Today I am helping you, tomorrow someone else will help me. "Act of kindness".

Parable or Saying: *ɛvri dɔg gɛt in de.*

Translation: *Every dog has his day.*

Interpretation: Everybody has his/her time to shine.

TODAY, NOW, AT THE MOMENT OR AT PRESENT

Parable or Saying: *Yu si tidɛ, yu nɔ si tumara. Tumara de ná God ĩ an.*

Translation: *You've seen today. Do not let anticipation of tomorrow be a burden on the day that is passing. Trust in the goodness of God.*

Interpretation: Hug tight today the one you love, your family and your friends; if tomorrow never comes, you will not have to regret today.

Parable or Saying: *Eg tidɛ bɛtɛ pas fɔl tumara.*

Translation: *An egg today is better than a hen tomorrow.*

Interpretation: An opportunity that you have today may not be available tomorrow.

TOGETHERNESS OR UNITY

Parable or Saying: *Fambul ná lɛkɛ tik bush; wɛ yu de ausai ĩ dak, ɛn wɛ yu de insai, ɛvri tik gɛt in yon ples.*

Translation: *A family is like a thick forest, often from the outside it is dense, and when you are inside, each tree has its own position.*

Interpretation: These are strong, loving family members; bound together by strong relationships, common interests, activities, rules and traditions to establish their way of life.

Parable or Saying: *Nɔ to wan pɔsin de mɛn pikin.*

Translation: *It takes a village to raise a child.*

Interpretation: The whole village community, extended family members and friends contribute in the upbringing of a child.

Parable or Saying: *Wɛ spaida in wɛb dɛm de togɛda, dèn kin tai layon.*

Translation: *When spider webs unite, they can tie up a lion.*

Interpretation: When people work together they can achieve much more than if one person tries to do everything.

Parable or Saying: *Ose tait sotɛ, fɔl de lay.*

Translation: *However tightly packed a house might be a hen will always find somewhere to lay her eggs.*

Interpretation: The state of being united or joined as a whole.

Parable or Saying: *Nɔ fred fɔ tɛl di lai wɛ go mek mared man ɛn ĩ wɛf de togɛda, bɔt nɔ tɛl di tru wɛ go skata dèm.*

Translation: *Don't hesitate to tell a lie that will unite husband and wife but don't tell the truth that will have them separated.*

Interpretation: That truth that will destroy a marriage, leave it unspoken. What therefore God hath joined together, let not man put asunder.

TOUGH, DANGEROUS OR RISKY

Parable or Saying: *Yu nɔ go skiad mɔŋki wit dai babu.*

Translation: *You cannot scare a monkey with a dead baboon.*

Interpretation: A fearless person with strong personality do not have to win but will not allow other people to walk all over him/her on the outside.

Parable or Saying: *Ná di kwayɛt wata ná in kin draun man.*

Translation: *It is the calm and silent water that drowns the man.*

Interpretation: Something that you expect to be safe can be more harmful and dangerous.

EYAMIDÉ ELLA LEWIS-COKER

TREACHEROUS, DECEITFUL, DISLOYAL, UNFAITHFUL OR UNTRUSTWORTHY

Parable or Saying: **Yu ná grin snek ná grin gras.**

Translation: *He or she is a green snake in a green grass.*

Interpretation: **A treacherous, deceitful, double-crossing or two-faced person who pretends to support you but secretly tries to harm you.**

Parable or Saying: **Ĩ ná lɛk rɔd, ĩ fayn bɔt in trik nɔ gud.**

Translation: *She is like a road, pretty and crooked.*

Interpretation: **A beautiful person with a bad character; deceives and misleads others.**

Parable or Saying: **Ĩ ná lɛk bugbug, wɛ de yit insai di wud ɛn den blɔ di wud.**

Translation: *He/she is like a termite that eats the inside of a wood and lives the outside untouched.*

Interpretation: **A dangerous, untruthful, deceitful or dishonest person.**

TRICKY, CRAFTY, CUNNING, DEVIOUS OR SLY

Parable or Saying: **Yu nɔ go tich ol dɔg niu trik.**

Translation: *You do not teach an old dog a new trick.*

Interpretation: **A cunning or skillful act intended to deceive or outwit someone.**

Parable or Saying:	**Mɔŋki nɔ de fɔgɛt ĩ blak an.**
Translation:	*A monkey does not forget the color of his hands.*
Interpretation:	**An act or procedure intended to achieve an end by deceptive or fraudulent means.**

Parable or Saying:	**Trik ná smok.**
Translation:	*Trick is smoke you cannot conceal it.*
Interpretation:	**A characteristic habit or mannerism that someone cannot hide.**

TROUBLE, DIFFICULTY, TRIAL, TRIBULATION, DILEMMA OR PROBLEM

Parable or Saying: *ɔl kondo lidɔm wit im bɛlɛ ná grɔn, nɔbɔdi nɔ no uz wan bɛlɛ de at.*

Translation: *All lizards lay flat on the ground, no one knows the one that is suffering from upset stomach.*

Interpretation: Be careful of people's outward appearance, no one knows their problems.

Parable or Saying: *Nɔ kam tɔn bon ɔ trɔbul ná mi trot.*

Translation: *Don't be difficult.*

Interpretation: A person who seems to make every situation toxic and impossible. A difficult person is not easy to be around and requires effort to maintain goodwill or to have his friendship.

Parable or Saying: *Nɔ tai ɔkpɔlɔ raun yu fut wɛ yu de rɔn pan snek.*

Translation: *Do not tie a frog around your foot while running from a snake.*

Interpretation: It's trouble!

Parable or Saying: *Udat trowɛ asis ná in asis kin fala.*

Translation: *Ashes always fly back into the face of the person who throws the ashes.*

Interpretation: Whatever you cause (good or bad), will have an effect on you.

Parable or Saying: *Udat di sus fit, lɛ ĩ wɛr am.*

Translation: *If the shoe fits you, wear it.*

Interpretation: An individual who is causing trouble has to deal with it.

Parable or Saying: *Wɛ yu mɔt kloz, flai nɔ go go insai.*

Translation: *If you close your mouth, fly will never get inside your mouth.*

Interpretation: If you learn when to keep silent you will avoid trouble.

Parable or Saying: *Wɛ yu nɔ waka usai faya de, faya nɔ go bɔn yu.*

Translation: *If you do not walk where there is fire, fire will not burn you.*

Interpretation: If you avoid trouble, trouble will not find you.

Parable or Saying: *Trɔbul nɔ de blɔ bigul wɛ ĩ de kam.*

Translation: *Trouble does not announce its arrival.*

Interpretation: Trouble does not happen at expected time. It is unforeseeable or uncertain.

Parable or Saying: *Mared man ná wahala.*

Translation: *A married man is a lot of trouble.*

Interpretation: Fooling around with a married man is a lot of trouble.

Parable or Saying: *Ren nɔ de fɔdɔm ná wan man dɔmɔt.*

Translation: *Rain does not fall on one man's roof.*

Interpretation: Trouble comes to everyone at one time or another.

Parable or Saying: *Ná ren de mek gɔt ɛn ship mit ná wan ɔndasɛla.*

Translation: *Unexpected rainfall allows goat and sheep to seek shelter under the same roof.*

Interpretation: Anything that causes difficulty and inconvenience, or that prevents someone from doing something.

Parable or Saying: *Eg nɔ gɛt ɛni biznɛs fɔ dans wit stonston.*

Translation: *Eggs have no business dancing with stones.*

Interpretation: Do not do anything with a person with whom you are not comfortable. It will be trouble!

Parable or Saying: *Nɔ gi mi wan fut.*

Translation: *Do not let me have just one foot.*

Interpretation: Do not involve someone in trouble.

Parable or Saying: *ɔg aks im mama wɛtin du im mɔt loŋ. Im mama sɛ nɔ wɔri mi pikin, wɛ yu big yu go si am fɔ yusɛf.*

Translation: *A pig asked his mom, "Mom why is your mouth so long?" His mother replied, "Don't worry child, you are growing up, you will see".*

Interpretation: Eventually every child will learn about the challenges of life.

Parable or Saying: *Pikin wɛ de ná im mama bak, nɔ no sɛ di rɔd fá.*

Translation: *A child on his/her mother's back will never realize that the road is long.*

Interpretation: The young and inexperienced don't understand true troubles or hardships.

Parable or Saying: *Wɛ kakroch mek dans, ĩ nɔ go invait fɔl.*

Translation: *When a roach is having a dance, he will never invite a rooster or hen.*

Interpretation: Don't invite trouble.

Parable or Saying: *Wɛ yu provok snek den yu go no sɛ ĩ kin tinap.*

Translation: *When you provoke a snake then you realize he/she can stand up.*

Interpretation: Don't invite problem or danger.

Parable or Saying: *Wɛ fɔl api, ak de nia.*

Translation: *If a rooster or hen is happy, hawk is near.*

Interpretation: Even in the happiest time one must be watchful.

Parable or Saying: *Wɛ fɔl de mek gladi gladi, ak de kam fɔ kach am.*

Translation: *When a rooster or hen is merry, a hawk will soon devour him/her.*

Interpretation: Danger lurks nearby when there is too much merriment and excitement.

Parable or Saying: *Nɔ trɔbul, trɔbul; tɛ trɔbul, trɔbul yu.*

Translation: *Do not trouble, trouble; until trouble, troubles you.*

Interpretation: Do not go looking for trouble.

Parable or Saying:	*ɛnibɔdi wɛ tot wɔk wɛ ĩ nɔ du fɔ tot yet, ĩ mɔs gɛt big trɔbul.*
Translation:	*Anyone who wants to do something that he/she is unprepared for is looking for trouble.*
Interpretation:	**Do not go looking for trouble.**

Parable or Saying:	***Udat mared fayn uman, mared wahala.***
Translation:	*He who marries a beauty marries trouble.*
Interpretation:	**Appearance can be deceptive.**

Parable or Saying:	***Wɛ wi gɛt wahala ɔ trɔbul wi mɛmba Gɔd.***
Translation:	*When we are in trouble we remember God.*
Interpretation:	**Since God in faithfulness remembers us, by faith we should remember God. No matter how difficult our trials, call upon him and wait patiently on God's timing.**

Parable or Saying:	***Ná trɔbul mek mɔŋki cham pɛpɛ.***
Translation:	*It is the trouble of the world that allows the monkey to chew hot, spicy pepper.*
Interpretation:	**People are forced to become innovative and resourceful under harsh conditions.**

Parable and Saying:	***Ston wɛ de bɔtɔm watasai nɔ no sɛ san ɔt.***
Translation:	*A stone at the bottom of the river does not know that the sun is hot.*
Interpretation:	**Sheltered person does not understand true hardship or trouble.**

Parable and Saying:	***Wahala ɔ trɔbul ful Oku blai.***
Translation:	*Trouble literally filled a basket known as Oku basket.*
Interpretation:	**A state of distress or dangerous situation.**

Parable or Saying: *ɛlifant ed nɔto pikin lod.*

Translation: *The elephant's head is no load for a child.*

Interpretation: When you're in trouble, anyway out is a good way out.

Parable or Saying: *ɔl krai du fɔ bɛrin.*

Translation: *Any kind of crying is appropriate at a funeral.*

Interpretation: Take whatever help you can when you are in trouble, even if it has some disadvantages.

TRUE, CORRECT, EXACT OR FACTUAL

Parable or Saying: **Da tru wɛ kin pwɛl mared, nɔ tɔk am.**

Translation: *The truth that can ruin a marriage, leave it unspoken.*

Interpretation: To be true to friends is to be compassionate in the sense of not telling them what they do not want to hear. If they have shown that they will react in ways that will hurt themselves and others, then it may be best not to tell them the truth.

TRUSTWORTHY, FAITHFUL, HONEST, RELIABLE OR TRUTHFUL

Parable or Saying: **Wɛ yu waŋ kip gud nɛba, lɔk yu dɔmɔt.**

Translation: *In order to keep your neighbor honest, lock your door.*

Intrepretation: The ability to rely on a reliable, truthful or trustworthy person.

UGLY OR UNPLEASANT

Parable or Saying: *Gɔd nɔ lɛk ɔgli ɔ wɔwɔ.*

Translation: *God do not like ugly.*

Interpretation: God does not like injustice. God will remember your bad deeds.

Parable or Saying: *Mɔŋki nɔba tink sɛ in pikin wɔwɔ.*

Translation: *A monkey never thinks her baby is ugly.*

Interpretation: Every mother thinks her child is the most beautiful child in the world.

UNAFRAID, BOLD, CONFIDENT, COURAGEOUS OR FEARLESS

Parable or Saying: *Wɛ arata de laf pus, ol de nia.*

Translation: *When the mouse laughs at the cat there is a hole nearby.*

Interpretation: A person who possesses or displays courage; able to face and deal with danger.

UNCONTROLLABLE, UNCONTAINABLE,

DISOBEDIENT OR DISORDERLY

Parable or Saying: *Wi de mach ɛn dans to di drɔm bit.*

Translation: *They are marching and dancing to the beat of the drum.*

Interpretation: People do things the way they want without taking other people into consideration.

Parable or Saying: *Wi de muv wi nɛk to di drɔm bit.*

Translation: *They are moving their necks according to the beat of the drum.*

Interpretation: They do things in their own way regardless of societal norms and conventional expectation.

UNDERSTAND, BE FAMILIAR WITH, GET THE PICTURE OR KNOW

Parable or Saying: *Ná Creole spun ná in gud fɔ tek pul Creole plasas sup.*

Translation: *It is the Creole spoon that is good to serve the Creole soup.*

Interpretation: A person who has clear-feeling, clear understanding or empathy for another person.

Parable or Saying: *Ná mɔŋki nɔmɔ de ɔndastan mɔŋki.*

Translation: *Only a monkey understands a monkey.*

Interpretation: A person who has the ability to understand, feel and share another person's emotions.

Parable or Saying: *Ná di nɛf nɔmɔ no aw di koko I insai luk lɛk.*

Translation: *Only a knife knows what the inside of a cocoyam looks like.*

Interpretation: Someone who understands or feels what another person is experiencing from within.

Parable or Saying: *Ná di sus sabi usai de pinch.*

Translation: *The shoe knows where the foot pinches.*

Interpretation: No one except the person who is feeling it knows the source or cause of the problem or difficulty.

Parable or Saying: *Ná di sus sabi wɛ di stɔkin gɛt ol.*

Translation: *The shoe knows if the stocking has a hole.*

Interpretation: No one but the individual who is experiencing it understands the reason or the problem.

UNGRATEFUL, THANKLESS, UNAPPRECIATIVE OR UNGRACIOUS

Parable or Saying: *Wɛ dɔg bɛt im masta, ĩ go bɛt trenja.*

Translation: *When a dog bites his master, he/she will bite a stranger.*

Interpretation: If your best friend is not accustomed of expressing thanks to you, he will do it to someone else.

Parable or Saying: *Nɔ bɛt di an wɛ de fid yu.*

Translation: *Do not bite the hand that feeds you.*

Interpretation: It is not a good idea to behave unkindly or ungratefully toward those on whom you depend for financial or other support.

Parable or Saying: *Nɔ tɛl di man wɛ de kɛr yu sɛ in ed de smɛl.*

Translation: *Do not tell a man who is carrying you that his head stinks.*

Interpretation: A person who does not have the feeling of exhibiting gratitude.

Parable or Saying:	*Udat dèn tot nɔ no sɛ rɔd fá.*
Translation:	*He who is carried does not realize the distance.*
Interpretation:	One who is privileged in some way does not realize how good he/she has it, compared to someone who does not have anything.

Parable or Saying:	*Udat dèn tɔt ná bak nɔ no sɛ di tɔŋ de fá.*
Translation:	*He who is carried on another's back does not appreciate how far off the town.*
Interpretation:	A person who is having financial assistance does not know the hardship in life and does not practice or exhibit an attitude of gratitude.

Parable or Saying:	*Pikin wɛ de ná im mama bak nɔ no sɛ di jɔni lɔŋ.*
Translation:	*A baby on her mother's back doesn't know that the journey is long.*
Interpretation:	A person who is supported does not know the hardship in life and does not practice or show a feeling of gratitude.

Parable or Saying:	*Nɔ kɔl di bush wɛ kɔba yu jɔnjul.*
Translation:	*Do not call the shrub over your shelter a jungle.*
Interpretation:	Do not insult someone who is capable of taking care of you.

Parable or Saying:	*Niu brum swip klin bɔt di ol brum no usai di dɔti de ná ɔl di kona.*
Translation:	*A new broom sweeps clean, but an old broom knows every corner.*
Interpretation:	A new leader with a new perspective can easily see where the old leadership missed some points and dealt with things that have been let go or over seen. However, the old leader knows his people and their habits and can easily take care of some situations with finesse because of aged wisdom.

UNSUCCESSFUL, DISASTROUS, FAILED, FRUITLESS OR UNPRODUCTIVE

Parable or Saying:	*Wɛ ɔkpɔlɔ nɔ gɛt tel wɛ ĩ yɔŋ, nɔto wɛ ĩ ol ĩ go gɛt tel.*
Translation:	*If a frog is without a tail during youth, it will take a miracle for it to acquire a tail at old age.*
Interpretation:	A person who is not achieving or is having an unfavorable outcome.

UNTRUSTWORTHY, DECEITFUL, DISLOYAL, UNDEPENDABLE OR UNRELIABLE

Parable or Saying:	*Wɛ yu liv bai di sod, yu go dai bai di sod.*
Translation:	*He that live by the sword will die by the sword.*
Interpretation	The way that you treat others is the way that others will treat you. People who commit violence must expect to receive violence.

Parable or Saying: *Tɛl yu sikrit tu bad kompin, ná lɛk wɛ yu put rɛs ná bag wɛ gɛt ol.*

Translation: *Confiding a secret to an unworthy person is like carrying grains in a bag with a hole.*

Interpretation: If you are going to tell a secret, tell it to someone you trust; otherwise the secret will no longer be secret, it will be known by everyone.

Parable or Saying: *Fisha-man ɔ fisha-uman nɔ go sɛ im fish rɔtin.*

Translation: *A fisherman or fisherwoman will not say his/her fish stinks or rots.*

Interpretation: A person who is not worthy of being trusted.

Parable or Saying: *Wɛ yu de fid pikin, yu gɛt fɔ tɛs di fud wit yu finga.*

Translation: *When you are feeding a child you have to taste the food with your fingers.*

Interpretation: A person who you cannot rely or depend upon.

Parable or Saying: *Bad uman go put mataodo ɛn pensul biɛn do inkes im man kam nak, "koŋk, koŋk"!*

Translation: *A deceitful woman will place a mortar and a pestle behind the door should her husband knocks.*

Interpretation: A deliberately misleading, cheating or deceptive person.

Parable or Saying: *Nɔ abop pan daiman sus, wɛ yu nɔ no ĩ siaz.*

Translation: *Do not depend on the dead man's shoes when you do not know his size.*

Interpretation: A person who place reliance or trust on someone.

Parable or Saying:	*Nɔ kɔnt yu fɔl pikin bifo dèn ach.*
Translation:	*Do not count your chicken before they are hatched.*
Interpretation:	Don't be certain for something that has not yet occurred.

Parable or Saying:	*Nɔ trai fɔ put ɔlman ed ná yoŋ-man sholda.*
Translation:	*Don't try to put old heads on young shoulders.*
Interpretation:	You can't expect a young person to have the wisdom or maturity associated with older person.

UNWELCOME, ANNOYING, UNDESIRABLE, UNINVITED OR UNWANTED

Parable or Saying:	*Yuba nɔ gɛt pepa bɔt ĩ no wɛn fɔtidɛ.*
Translation:	*A vulture without an invitation for an African feast, welcomed himself.*
Interpretation:	A guest or new arrival who is not needed or not gladly received in any situation. "An unwanted guest".

UNWISE, FOOLISH OR STUPID

Parable or Saying:	*Ná fulman go put in tu fut fɔ tɛs aw di wata dip ná watasai.*
Translation:	*Only a fool tests the depth of water with both feet.*
Interpretation:	It is not wise to jump into a situation before thinking about it.

Parable or Saying:	*Ná fulman go klem lɛda wɛ ĩ an dèm de ná im pɔkit.*
Translation:	*Only a fool climbs a ladder with both hands in the pocket.*
Interpretation:	When you're unsure of something or uncertain you shouldn't jump right into it.

USE, CUSTOM, HABIT, USAGE, USELESS OR PRACTICE

Parable or Saying:	*Dɔti wata sɛf kin ɔt faya.*
Translation:	*Dirty or filthy water could be utilized to put out a fire.*
Interpretation:	Everything has its use.

WALK, STROLL OR TOTTER

Parable or Saying:	*Lan fɔ crip bifo yu waka.*
Translation:	*Learn to crawl before you walk.*
Interpretation:	A person learns the basics before he/she tries to do things that are more complexed. Take things one step at a time.

WANT, DESIRE OR NEED

Parable or Saying:	*Waŋt, waŋt nɔ gɛt; gɛt, gɛt nɔ waŋt.*
Translation:	*People who really want something can't achieve them, those who are getting things do not want them.*
Interpretation:	Have nots covet what the haves take for granted.

Parable or Saying:	*Wilful wes, mek woful want.*
Translation:	*Wilful waste makes woeful want.*
Interpretation:	If you waste what you have, soon you will not have anything.

WATCHOUT, BE ALERT, BE CAREFUL, BE-CAUTIOUS OR LOOK OUT

Parable or Saying:	*Put tik biɛn yu do wɛ yu nɛba in dɔg go kres.*
Translation:	*Place a stick behind your door in case your neighbor's dog gets mad.*
Interpretation:	Watching or observing someone or something closely and be on the look out for danger.

Parable or Saying:	*Wɛ kak drɔŋk, ĩ fɔgɛt sɛ ak de.*
Translation:	*When a cock or rooster is drunk, he forgets about the hawk.*
Interpretation:	One should always be on the alert in life. It is warning to people who get out of a circumstance and forget about it. It is always good for one to remember that whatever threatens one's life never goes away, regardless of one's circumstances.

WEALTH, ABUNDANCE, CAPITAL OR PROSPERITY

Parable or Saying:	*Jɛntri nɔ kam bai takiti.*
Translation:	*Gentry does not derive by hard working.*
Interpretation:	Gentry or aristocrats are people of social or specified class whose income derives from estates.

Parable or Saying:	***Banana dòn gɛt wata bifo rɛn kam.***
Translation:	*The banana plant always has water even if it does not rain.*
Interpretation:	**A wealthy person will always be wealthy if even the economy booms or slumps; he does not have to worry.**

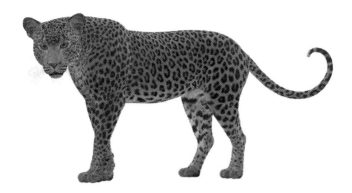

WISDOM, GOOD JUDGEMENT, INSIGHT, INTELLIGENCE OR KNOWLEDGE

Parable or Saying: **Wɛ lɛpɛt sok, ná im dèn animal dèm go ple nia di aria.**

Translation: *It is when a leopard is wet that animals will play around.*

Interpretation: A person who has the ability to think using knowledge and experience to make good decisions.

Parable or Saying: **Mina nɔ de swim ná di sem dip sai pan di wata lɛk bonita.**

Translation: *Minnow does not swim in the same depth of water as the Bonita.*

Interpretation: A person with common sense or good judgement.

Parable or Saying: **Kɔt yu kot akɔdin tu yu klos.**

Translation: *Cut your coat according to your cloth.*

Interpretation: Match your actions to your resources, and do not try to live beyond your means.

Parable or Saying: *Gɔt go kik lɛpɛt wɛ ĩ gɛt romatisim.*

Translation: *A goat will kick a leopard when the leopard is suffering from rheumatism/arthritis.*

Interpretation: An individual with the ability to discern right from wrong.

Parable or Saying: *Dɔg ná gud kɔnsibul bɔt ĩ nɔ go patrɔl ná di trit wɛ lɛpɛt tap.*

Translation: *Dog is an effective constable but he won't patrol in the street where the Leopard lives.*

Interpretation: Think twice! Don't dare to fit in where you don't belong.

Parable or Saying: *Man wɛ no parɛbul kin sɛtul plaba.*

Translation: *A wise man who knows proverbs can reconcile difficulties.*

Interpretation: If you can understand the lesson behind a proverb, you will understand where your problems begin and how to resolve them.

Parable or Saying: *Ná di sus sabi wɛ di stɔkin gɛt ol.*

Translation: *The shoe knows if the stocking has a hole.*

Interpretation: No one but the individual who is experiencing it knows the reason of the problem.

Parable or Saying: *Ná di gɔm sabi wɛtin di tit de du.*

Translation: *The gum understands the teeth affairs.*

Interpretation: No one but the person who comes in contact with an individual knows the situation.

WITHSTAND, BEAR UP, ENDURE, HOLD OUT, HOLD UP, SURVIVE OR SUSTAIN

Parable or Saying: *Uman ampa nɔ de fɔdɔm.*

Translation: *Nothing holds a woman back or nothing will get into a woman's way.*

Interpretation: A female will pull through to sustain herself, in spite of danger or hardship.

WOMAN, FEMALE OR LADY

Parable or Saying: *Wɛ yu nɔ lɛk uman dem wɛ de tɔk tɔk ɛn kongosa, dèn bi palampo.*

Translation: *If don't like chattering women, stay a bachelor.*

Interpretation: Women who talk too much about meaningless things are very annoying to men and obviously turn men off from relationships. Men expect women to speak only when it is meaningful.

Parable or Saying: *Udat mared fayn uman, mared wahala.*

Translation: *He who marries a beauty marries trouble.*

Interpretation: Appearance can be deceptive.

Parable or Saying: *Uman mɔt nɔ gɛt blo blo.*

Translation: *The mouth of a woman takes no holiday.*

Interpretation: However, a woman will only talk a lot if she enjoys the person's company she is keeping at that moment. She wants the person to be more involved in and aware of her life. On the other hand, if the person remains quiet and just nod his/ her head, it will seem that the woman talks a lot.

Parable or Saying:	*Om wɛ nɔ gɛt uman ná lɛk ɛmti ship ose wɛ ship nɔ tap.*
Translation:	*A home without a woman is like a barn without cattle.*
Interpretation:	A home without a woman is depressing, cheerless or joyless and no one is there to be of assistance.

WORK, DETERMINATION OR LABOR

Parable or Saying:	*ɔs nɔ tu gud fɔ tot in gras.*
Translation:	*Horse is not too good to carry his/her own grass.*
Interpretation:	One who takes a survival job to help pay the bills.

Parable or Saying:	*Natin nɔ izi.*
Translation:	*Nothing comes easy.*
Interpretation:	Strive very hard to accomplish your goals.

Parable or Saying:	*Wɔk ná mɛrɛsin fɔ po man.*
Translation:	*Work is the medicine for poverty.*
Interpretation:	Work very hard to be the greatest.

WORRY, ANXIETY, BE ANXIOUS,
BOTHER OR CONCERN

Parable or Saying:	*Lɛ ĩ go, lɛk wata ná dɔks bak.*
Translation:	*Let it go like water on duck's back.*
Interpretation:	A person who has the ability to let go of criticisms or negative events because he/she is uanaffected by such things.

Parable and Saying:	*Nɔ gi mi wan fut.*
Translation:	*Don't let me give in to worry or anger; it only leads to trouble.*
Interpretation:	**A state that will cause anxiety, nervousness, worry or fear.**

Parable and Saying:	*Tit nɔ de munin.*
Translation:	*Smiling with visible teeth and worried at the same time.*
Interpretation:	**You appear happy to everyone, but you are actually stressed.**

Parable and Saying:	*Gɔd nɔ de slip.*
Translation:	*Cast your cares on the Almighty, he will be up all night anyway.*
Interpretation:	**Turn all your worries to the Lord because he cares for you. He will graciously guide and protect you.**

ACKNOWLEDGEMENTS

I would like to express my gratitude to all those who gave me the incentive in writing the second edition of *"Creoles Of Sierra Leone Proverbs♦Parables♦Wise Sayings"* with literal English translations and interpretations.

A special thanks to those who provided support, discussed things over, read, wrote, offered comments, and assisted me in editing, proofreading and designing.

I am deeply indebted to some of my departed family: My grandmother, father, mother, bothers, sisters, uncles, aunts and cousins. My thanks for their constant encouragement in enabling me to publish this book. Above all, I want to say special thanks to my husband, sons, grand-children and siblings for supporting and encouraging me in spite of all the time it took me away from them. It was a long and difficult journey!

Last but not least, I would like to say thanks and appreciation to the rest of my family, not forgotten the brothers and sisters of Sierra Leone for their contributions in the process of selecting and editing this book.

ABOUT THE AUTHOR

Mrs. Eyamidé E. Lewis-Coker: Retired Lecturer, Certified Lay Minister at First United Methodist Church, Ontario, California and President of Creole Heritage Organization in California was born and raised in Freetown, Sierra Leone, West Africa.

Says the author, "I have been an expertise in West African proverbs, parables and wise sayings since the age of six. I share my knowledge during discussions and conversations using ancestral proverbs, parables and wise sayings to point out and convey the truth in an easily understandable way. I utilize these proverbs, parables and wise sayings pointing out where others have failed and helping others to avoid the same mistakes. I also utilize proverbs to describe actions, show results, dilemmas and consequences of choices made by people in their daily lives". These ancestral proverbs, parables and wise sayings are the essential vehicles that transmit African wisdom, morals, traditions and values.

Mrs. Eyamidé E. Lewis-Coker resides in the United States. This is the author's fourth full-length published book

Printed in the United States
By Bookmasters